Impressum

1. Auflage Juni 1992 *First Edition June 1992*

Herausgeber *Publisher*
Waechtersbacher Keramik
Otto Friedrich Fürst zu Ysenburg
und Büdingen GmbH & Co. KG.
6486 Brachttal

Idee und Konzept *Idea and Concept*
Michael Graf Praschma

Realisation und Redaktion *Edited by*
Transparent Design Management GmbH, Frankfurt

Gestaltung *Design*
Designgruppe Transparent, Kiel

Autoren *Authors*
Elisabeth Budde
Prof. Dr. Michael Erlhoff
Michael Graf Praschma
Petra Schmidt

Übersetzung *Translation*
Dr. Jeremy Gaines
Paul Keast

Fotografie *Photography*
Ad Berger, Bad Soden
Angela Francisca Endress und
Michael Tessmann, Frankfurt

Lithographie *Reproduction*
Brandner, Kiel

Druck *Printed by*
Nieswand Druck, Kiel

Verlag *Published by*
Nieswand Verlag, Kiel

Umschlag *Cover*
Schale von Elizabeth Garouste und Mattia Bonetti,
1991 für Waechtersbacher Keramik.
Bowl by Elizabeth Garouste and Mattia Bonetti,
1991 for Waechtersbacher Keramik.

Printed in Germany

ISBN 3-926048-90-5

Colour Comedies

Internationaler Architekten- und Designer-Workshop der Waechtersbacher Keramik

Michael Graves
Zaha Hadid
Elizabeth Garouste und Mattia Bonetti
Atsushi Kitagawara
Jo Laubner
Ettore Sottsass

INHALT / *CONTENT*

PROF. DR. MICHAEL ERLHOFF
Einführung / *Introduction* Seite / *Page* 6

GAROUSTE UND BONETTI
Seite / *Page* 8

MICHAEL GRAVES
Seite / *Page* 18

ZAHA. M. HADID
Seite / *Page* 24

ATSUSHI KITAGAWARA
Seite / *Page* 35

JO LAUBNER
Seite / *Page* 40

ETTORE SOTTSASS
Seite / *Page* 49

WAECHTERSBACHER KERAMIK
Seite / *Page* 60

BIBLIOGRAFIE / *BIBLIOGRAPHY*
Seite / *Page* 64

Vorab muß zu dieser Dokumentation unseres Workshops einfach gesagt werden, wieviel Freude dabei war: die Freude über die Bereitwilligkeit aller mitzumachen, angefangen bei der großen organisatorischen Leistung, dann die spontane Bereitschaft der Workshop-Teilnehmer und insbesondere die hingebungsvolle, aufopfernde Arbeit bei der Realisation der vielen so individuellen Entwürfe. Nur wer Kenntnis von der handwerklich anspruchsvollen Steingut-Herstellung hat und über Formenbau und Glasurenentwicklung weiß, kann nachvollziehen, welche Schwierigkeiten hier scheinbar mühelos überwunden wurden.
Allen Mitwirkenden gilt deshalb mein besonderer Dank.

Die Waechtersbacher Keramik ist vielfältig. Ein 160 Jahre altes Unternehmen, das immer einen individuellen Weg gegangen ist, ausbalanciert zwischen Tradition und Wahrung eines Waechtersbach-typischen Stils einerseits und einer zeitgemäßen Weiterentwicklung andererseits.

Waechtersbach, das ist eine große Produktpalette, das sind Farben, das ist Freude am Schenken und am Tischdecken mit einem Spritzer frischer, modischer Raffinesse, alles in allem: Lebensfreude und Spaß haben.
Idee des Workshops war es deshalb, diesen Charakter und die hohe Leistungsfähigkeit in der Herstellung von hochwertigem farbigem Steingut mit einer Auswahl der international renommiertesten Architekten und Designer durch ungewöhnliche, kreative und sehr anspruchsvolle Arbeiten zu demonstrieren.
Was wir nicht wollten, war die Realisation eines soundsovielten "Designer-Programms". Vielmehr war – auch den Workshop-Teilnehmern – der Spaß an der Idee wichtig, sich mit mehreren anderen Gestaltern zusammenzusetzen und sich mit einer ungewöhnlichen Aufgabe und einem Material zu beschäftigen, mit dem die Teilnehmer nicht jeden Tag arbeiten.

Die Aufgabe lautete dementsprechend, wie der Titel schon ausdrückt: Die Designer sollen bei ihrer Arbeit soviel Spaß haben wie möglich. Wir wollen bei der Entwicklung, der Realisation und bei der Präsentation Spaß haben, und wir möchten, daß das Publikum Spaß hat beim Betrachten der Ergebnisse.
In diesem Sinne wünsche ich auch dem Betrachter dieses Buches viel Freude.

What more fitting way to preface this documentary record of our workshop than simply to say how much pleasure it has given: pleasure at the willingness shown by all concerned, starting with the magnificent achievement of those in charge of organization, then the spontaneous enthusiasm of the workshop participants themselves and in particular the dedicated, painstaking work that went into the realization of the many highly individual designs. Only those with inside knowledge of the craftsman's skills involved in producing exclusive ceramics, in constructing the moulds and developing the glazes, will be fully able to appreciate the levels of difficulty that have been mastered here with apparent ease.
I would therefore like to express my sincerest thanks to all who contributed.

There are many sides to Waechtersbacher Keramik. A company of 160 years' standing, always prepared to go its own way, maintaining an even balance between, on the one hand, adherence to tradition and the typical Waechtersbacher style, and on the other, the need to develop contemporary innovations.

The name Waechtersbacher stands for a wide range of products, for colour, for the pleasure that comes from presenting a gift or laying the table with items that have a dash of refined and refreshing style. In short, Waechtersbacher is part of enjoying life.

The idea behind the workshop was therefore to demonstrate these characteristics and to show the heights that can be scaled in the manufacture of high grade colour-glazed ceramics. For this purpose, we invited a select group of the world's most respected architects and designers to produce unusual, creative and highly ambitious designs.

The last thing we wanted was to produce yet another "designer line". For us, and for the workshop participants themselves, the real interest lay in being able to savour the fun of sitting down with fellow designers, of getting to grips with an unusual assignment and with a material which is not normally part of their everyday work.

As the title of the workshop suggests, their brief was therefore to get as much fun out of their work as possible. We wanted to have fun developing, producing and presenting the pieces, and we hope that the public will have just as much fun viewing the results. With this in mind, I hope the reader of this book will find it too a lasting source of pleasure.

PROF. MICHAEL ERLHOFF

ERGREIFENDES UND BEGREIFENDES ÜBER FARBE UND KERAMIK

Angesichts der an diesem Workshop Beteiligten und ihrer Ergebnisse fällt wohltuend auf: Sie sind farbenfroh, also nicht bunt.
Denn bunt sind nur Hunde, und die sind schwarzweiß gefleckt, wirken also – wie alle Buntheit – nur grau und eintönig. Bunte Ensembles nämlich erscheinen öde und leer, als das Tohuwabohu oder als der Schrecken der Langeweile und verkleistern damit lediglich die Trauer über den Verlust von Erkenntnis und Differenz, der uns zunehmend allesamt erfaßt. Denn das Bunte ist sich stets ähnlich.

Grau in Grau verzerrt den Unterschied und verschwimmt vor den Augen zur Seelenlosigkeit. Farbe dagegen fordert die Distinktion, lädt Entwurf und Betrachtung zur Entschlossenheit ein und demonstriert den Willen zum Eigensinn. Sie konstruiert und sprengt auf, sie schafft Transparenz assoziativer Logik und zertrümmert jede Statik: Farbe eröffnet Perspektiven, insistiert auf der Vielfalt des Möglichen und demaskiert die Lüge jeder infamen Uniformität und Vereinheitlichung. Mit Farben werden Widersprüche gestaltet, sie sind der Wein und die Pasteten von Revolten.

Dabei hat der Einsatz von Farbe in der Gestaltung viele voneinander geschiedene und dennoch oft ineinander verwobene Facetten. Mal dient sie quasi pädagogischen Maßnahmen, materiale Aufmerksamkeit zu erregen (Feuerlöscher sind eben rot), mal schafft sie die optische Zerstörung der Gestalt eines Gegenstands oder einer Person, ein anderes Mal ist sie Zitat oder nur Unterscheidungsversuch und Zeichen der Suche nach Identität, machmal gar verstrickt sie sich in der Hoffnung auf eine gültige und kommunizierbare Symbolik. Denn die, die mit ihr gestalten, spielen immer mit der Psyche der die Arbeit Betrachtenden und fallen dabei meist der eigenen Psychologie zum Opfer; sie gestalten Farbe bewußt oder unbewußt allemal im Rahmen und als Rahmen kultureller Ausdrucksformen, denen man folgen kann, die aber ebensogut neu etabliert oder auch ins Utopische transformiert werden können. Deshalb gehört Farbe zur Substanz von Alltagskultur und spielt die Rolle von Knoten im gesellschaftlichen Beziehungsgeflecht (was übrigens auch Chemiker im Rahmen ihrer Analysen und Reagenzien bestätigen), – wie Saul Blöchmer häufig zitierte: "Kultur ist der Fußabdruck vielfarbiger Beziehungen".

Nun, bekanntlich wird das Alltägliche durch Farben eben belebt und sind Farben für das Auge wiederum das, was für die Hände die Haptik ist. Gewissermaßen tasten die Augen die Farben ab, halten sie sich an einzelnen fest, wandern sie an ihnen entlang. Nicht unversehens formulierte in den zwanziger Jahren ein durchaus ernsthafter Philosoph in der enthusiastischen Nachfolge Immanuel Kants das Sehen als "excentrische Empfindung".

Begreifen wir aber das Sehen von Farben als gleichsam haptischen Vorgang, dann wiederum liegt als Farbträger das Material Keramik sehr nahe, ist dies doch eines der alltäglich greifbarsten, fast ein Synonym für das Erfassen. Denn Keramik vermittelt die Erfahrung des Stofflichen, eines ertastbaren Volumens, das bei aller schließlichen Glätte immer noch genügend Anhaltspunkte gibt, mit den Händen parallel zu den Augen zu arbeiten, das Gewicht und die Struktur des Gegenstandes zu verstehen. – Womit zweifellos immer auch ein Moment der Nachahmung des Schöpfungsaktes oder des Schaffensprozesses gerade von Keramiken verbunden ist.

Betrachten wir also abschließend die Arbeiten der an diesem Workshop Beteiligten, so finden wir all diese Momente der farbigen Keramik wieder: den lustvollen Umgang, das Zitat, den kulturellen Vergleich, die Dekonstruktion, die Liebe zum Material, die Gleichgültigkeit der Farben und das Glück des Gestaltens. Zaha Hadid zum Beispiel besänftigt – analog zu den unscharfen Kanten von Keramik – die Farben, holt sie aus der Eindeutigkeit des Konstruktiven heraus und schafft so einen Kontrast zur theoretischen Härte der Flächen ihrer Arbeit, Kitagawara paraphrasiert bekannte architektonische Formen und vergoldet sie, und Michael Graves beschwichtigt die von ihm zitierte Monumentalität der Architektur und umgibt sich zugleich mit dem auratischen Schein romantischer Utopie. Ettore Sottsass vergnügt sich in der Reformulierung und behutsamen Veränderung von älteren seiner Entwürfe, wobei die Farben demonstrativ gebrochener oder vielschichtiger werden, Garouste und Bonetti egalisieren, erhöhen und sortieren die formal amorphen und für uns kaum nachvollziehbar erscheinenden Applikationen ihrer Objekte mit farblicher Transparenz, während Laubner das Pathos der Symbolik so sehr erhöht, daß es wieder gewöhnlich wird.

Jede Arbeit steht für sich und ist zugleich Exempel für die Fortschreibung der Geschichte farbiger Keramik – und für unsere Hoffnung, den Sinnen manchmal doch noch trauen zu können.

PROF. MICHAEL ERLHOFF

ON GRASPING COLOUR AND CERAMICS

In view of the people participating in this workshop and what they have come up with, one thing pleases the eye: they are full of gorgeous colour and are not just colourful.

After all, in a pack of mongrels a Dalmatian might stick out, but it itself is only black and white and thus actually just gray and monotonous – and things are no different with all colourfulness. For any use of a multitude of colours is simply tedious and devoid of content, amounting to chaos or stemming from a fear of boredom, serving only to mask the sorrow we feel over a loss of both knowledge and a sense of difference, a loss increasingly befalling us all. For one batch of colourfulness is always similar to another, merely gray on gray, distorting difference and blurring before our eyes into soullessness.

Colour, by contrast, calls for distinctions to be made, encourages the project to be incisive and the viewer to be decisive, as well as demonstrating a will to be stubbornly idiosyncratic. Colour constructs while at the same time bursting things wide open, creating transparency via associative logic and sweeping things into movement: Colour opens up perspectives, insisting on the wealth of possibilities and exposing all uniformity and standardization to be an infamous lie. Colours lend shape to contradictions, they are the manna of revolt.

There are many different and yet nevertheless often interrelated facets to the use of colour in design. Sometimes colour serves some didactic purpose as it were, arousing interest in the materials involved (fire extinguishers just happen to be red), and at other times it functions to destroy the shape of an object or person. Yet again, it may merely be a quotation or an attempt to set something off from others, a sign of a search for identity; alternatively, it may be bound up with some hope that a valid symbolism can thus be created which can be communicated to the onlooker. After all, those who design by using colours are always simultaneously playing with the psyche of the person viewing the work in question and are thus usually a victim of their own psychology. Whatever the case, they consciously or unconsciously design colour in a specific framework, and as the frame for forms of cultural expression – forms one can adopt from a tradition but which one can just as easily establish for the first time or transform into something utopian. As a consequence, colour is part of the bedrock of everyday culture and functions as a point of interchange in the web of social relations (something chemists have confirmed in the context of their analyses and tests). Saul Blöchmer frequently alluded to this when he said: "Culture is the footprint of multi-coloured relations." As we all know, everyday life is energized by the presence of colours and colours are to the eyes what hands are to touch: to a certain extent, eyes feel their way along the colours, come to rest on one or the other, wandering across their surfaces. It was no coincidence that in the twenties and enthusiastically following in the train of Kant's thought a quite serious philosopher construed vision as "eccentric sensation."

If we, by contrast, understand the act of seeing colours to also be a haptic process, then ceramics as the bearer of colour suggests itself as a material, for it is one of the most tangible everyday properties, almost a synonym for something we quite literally grasp. Ceramics conveys the feel of being something tangible, a volume that the fingers can trace and which for all its final smoothness still gives observers sufficient cause to use their hands and eyes simultaneously in order to understand the weight and structure of the object. — Without doubt, precisely ceramics involves an element of imitating the act of creation or the process of production.

If we, in conclusion, cast a glance over the works produced by the participants in this workshop then we encounter all these elements of colourful ceramics: a playfulness, quotations, cultural comparisons, deconstruction, a love of the material, the equivalence of the colours and the joy of shaping. Zaha Hadid, for example, soothes the colours – in analogy to the softer edges of the ceramics – teasing them out of the clarity of constructiveness and thus creating a contrast to the theoretical hardness of the surfaces of her works. Kitagawara paraphrases well-known architectonic forms and covers them in gold. Michael Graves appeases the monumentality of architecture which he quotes and surrounds himself with the auratic glow of a Romantic utopia. Ettore Sottsass enjoys reformulating and carefully changing his older designs, in which process the colours become demonstratively more fragmented and many-layered. Garouste and Bonetti neutralize, intensify and classify the formally amorphous applications of their objects, applications we observers can hardly comprehend, with a transparency of colour – and last but not least Laubner takes the pathos of symbolism to such heights that it becomes quite commonplace again.

Each work represents only itself and yet is at the same time an example for both the ongoing historiography of coloured ceramics and the hope that we will, on occasion, be able to trust our senses.

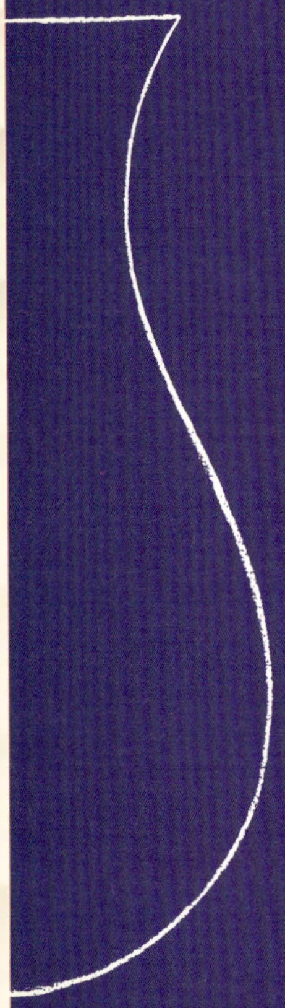

ELIZABETH GAROUSTE UND MATTIA BONETTI

Elizabeth Garouste
Elizabeth Garouste wurde 1949 in Paris geboren. Heute lebt sie mit ihrem Ehemann, dem Maler Gérard Garouste und ihren beiden Kindern auf ihrem Anwesen "La Mésangère" in der Normandie.

Mattia Bonetti
Mattia Bonetti ist 1952 in Lugano geboren. Er blieb zunächst in der Schweiz und absolvierte eine Schule für angewandte Kunst. Erst später kam er nach Paris, wo er heute noch lebt.

Das Team Garouste und Bonetti
1979 arbeiteten sie zum ersten Male gemeinsam beim Ausbau des Privatclubs "Privilège" der Pariser Diskothek "Le Palace". 1982 wurden sie endgültig Partner.

Ihre erste Einzelausstellung "Barbare" hatten sie schon im Jahre 1981 im Einrichtungshaus Jansen in Paris. Ihre Arbeit 1986 war Gegenstand der Ausstellungen im Victoria and Albert Museum in London, der Düsseldorfer Ausstellung "Wohnen von Sinnen" und der "Biennale" in Venedig.

1987 begann die Zusammenarbeit mit Christian Lacroix, dessen Boutiquen und Firmensitz sie gestalteten. Für den französischen Glashersteller "Daum" entwarfen sie 1989 die "Trapani" Kollektion, bestehend aus Besteckserie, Tafelservice, Spiegeln und Kleinmöbeln. 1990 erarbeiteten sie im Auftrag des Fürstenhauses von Thurn und Taxis die gesamte Inneneinrichtung für das Regensburger Schloßcafé. Eine Flaconkollektion entwarfen die beiden 1991 für Nina Ricci, Paris.

Elizabeth Garouste
Elizabeth Garouste was born in Paris in 1949. Today she lives with her husband, the painter Gérard Garouste, and their two children at "La Mésangère", their estate in Normandy.

Mattia Bonetti
Mattia Bonetti was born in Lugano in 1952. He initially remained in Switzerland, where he attended an academy for the applied arts. Later, he moved to Paris, where he still lives today.

The Garouste and Bonetti Team
The two first collaborated in 1979 when they worked jointly on the "Privilège" private club, an extension to the Paris discotheque "Le Palace". In 1982 they finally became partners.

In 1981 they opened their first joint show entitled "Barbare" at the Jansen interior design store in Paris. In 1986 their objects were also the subject of exhibitions at the London Victoria and Albert Museum, the Düsseldorf "Wohnen von Sinnen" show, and the Venice Biennial. 1987 marked the beginning of their collaboration with couturier Christian Lacroix, whose boutiques and company headquarters they designed. They worked for "Daum", the French glass manufacturer, in 1989, designing the "Trapani" collection consisting of cutlery set, tableware, mirrors and small items of furniture. In 1990, they worked for the royal Thurn und Taxis family designing the overall interior of the café at Schloß Regensburg. And as recently as 1991 they created a series of perfume flacons for Nina Ricci of Paris.

Kommode "Belgravia", 1990.
Entworfen für die Galerie Néotù Editions.
"Belgravia" chest of drawers, 1990.
Designed for the Néotù Editions Gallery.

Interieur des Regensburger Schloßcafés für das Fürstenhaus von Thurn und Taxis, 1990.
Café interior at Regensburg Castle for the Thurn and Taxis family, 1990.

Schrank "Sévres", 1989.
Hergestellt von der "Manufacture Nationale de Sévres" und der Galerie "Néotù", Paris und New York.
"Sévres" cupboard, 1989.
Produced by Manufature Nationale de Sévres and Néotù Gallery, Paris and New York.

"Ihr Barbarismus korrespondiert sehr gut mit meinem Geschmack für das Merkwürdige und Bizarre. Ich schätze die Sinnlichkeit, solange sie ungehindert bleibt"[1], sagt der französische Couturier Christian Lacroix zur Arbeit des Designerteams Garouste und Bonetti.

Mit dem Barbarismus fing alles an. Der Begriff leitet sich von "Barbare" ab, ihrer ersten Möbelkollektion, die sie 1981 in Paris zeigten. Sie präsentierten Möbel aus grob bearbeitetem Eisen, patiniert und mit Tierfell bezogen. Die Objekte wirkten wie Kultgegenstände einer archaischen Gesellschaft. Eine einzigartige Ungezogenheit gegenüber dem damals herrschenden Geschmack des High-Techs und der unterkühlten Interieurs. Die Fachpresse jedoch war begeistert.

Natürlich haben sich ihre Themen im Laufe der Jahre verändert. Immer mehr wurden Stile thematisiert und neu interpretiert, die ihrem Interesse an sinnlich anmutender Dekoration und dramatischen Inszenierungen Raum boten. Die gesamte Menschheits- und Kulturgeschichte dient ihnen hierbei als Bühne für ihr raffiniertes Spiel mit Zitaten und Versatzstücken.

"Their barbarianism corresponds well to my taste of the strange and bizarre. I value sensuality when it is unhindered"[1], says French fashion mogul Christian Lacroix of the work of the Garouste and Bonetti design team.

And it was barbarianism that everything started. The concept derives from "barbarian", their first furniture collection which they put on show in Paris in 1981. They presented furniture made of coarsely processed iron, patinated and covered with hide. The result was furniture with the feel of a cultic object from an archaic society about it.

This was uniquely naughty given the prevalent high-tech taste of the day and the predominance of subdued cool interiors. Yet the specialist journals were openly enthusiastic.

Needless to say, the themes Garouste and Bonetti address have changed over the years. Increasingly, they have topicalized particular styles and submitted them to new interpretations, styles that gave scope to their interest in both decoration with a sensuous flair and dramatic scenery. In this context, the whole cultural history of humankind serves as their stage for a highly intricate game of quotation and set pieces.

Kollektion "Barbare", 1981.
From the "Barbare" collection, 1981.

Immer neue Anklänge an immer andere Richtungen der Stilgeschichte treten im schnellen Wechsel in ihr kompositorisches Rampenlicht. Mit größter Selbstverständlichkeit verwenden sie Anleihen an das Mittelalter, die afrikanische Kunst, den venezianischen Barock, den Neo-Klassizismus, ja, sogar an die Moderne. Der Charakter und die Konsequenz im Umgang mit diesen Stilen sind zu ihrem unverkennbaren Markenzeichen geworden.

Der bereits erwähnte Christian Lacroix hat selbst durch extravagante Kreationen in der Pariser Modewelt für Furore gesorgt und fühlt sich bei dem Designerpaar in guten Händen. Er beauftragte die beiden mit der Innenausstattung all seiner Boutiquen im In- und Ausland, seines Firmensitzes in Paris und der Gestaltung von Flacons für seine Parfums.

Their compositions are constantly spotlighting new references to yet another traditional stylistic direction in rapid succession. As if it were quite usual, they incorporate elements from sources as divergent as the Middle Ages, African art, the Venetian Baroque, Neoclassicism, indeed even modernism. The way they make use of these styles, and the consistency with which they do so, have become their unmistakable hallmark.

Christian Lacroix, already mentioned above and who himself has caused a veritable furore in the Paris fashion world with truly extravagant creations, feels his cause is in good hands when entrusted to them. He commissioned them with the interior design of all his boutiques in France and abroad, as well as his Paris headquarters, and also with the design of flacons for his perfumes.

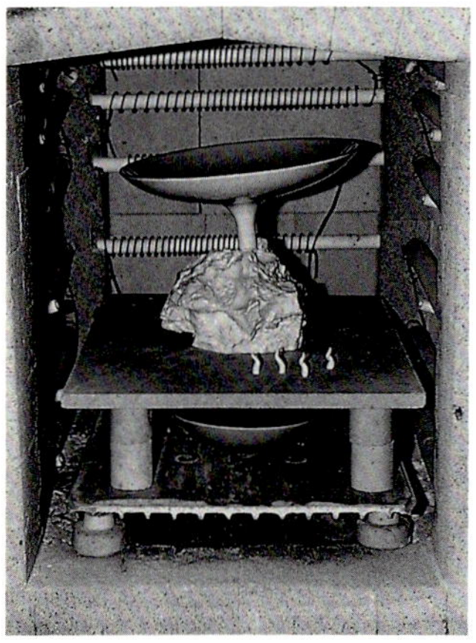

Bei der Realisierung wurde sogar die grobe Beschaffenheit des Lava-Gesteins von den Formenbauern exakt nachempfunden.
Even the coarse texture of the igneous rock was imitated perfectly by the mould constructors.

Mattia Bonetti bei der Besprechung der Entwürfe. Die Steine sammelte er auf seinen Spaziergängen.
Mattia Bonetti discussing his designs. He collected the stones while out walking.

Bei diesem kostbar anmutenden Pokal ist das Thema der "nature sophistiqueé", der verfälschten Natur, besonders gegenwärtig. Aus der unbearbeiteten, schroffen Form eines Natursteins wächst auf einem schmalen Stiel die eigentliche Obstschale. Durch die applizierten Keramikknospen und den verschwenderischen Umgang mit den Farben Blau und Gold entstand ein Gefäß, das Assoziationen an den Prunk längst versunkener Königreiche entstehen läßt.
Maße: ø 25,9 cm, 21 cm hoch

This large, expensive looking goblet stresses the theme of "nature sophistiquée" particularly strongly. The fruit bowl proper rises up on a tender stem out of a jagged piece of rock, left unaltered. The applied ceramic buds and the extravagant use of the colours blue and gold have generate a vessel which triggers associations with the sumptuous glory of latter-day kingdoms.
ø 25.9 cm, height: 21 cm

Die bekannte klassische Vasenform hat hier ein für Garouste und Bonetti typisches Dekor erhalten.
The well-known classical vase shape is furnished with decor typical of Garouste and Bonetti.

Entstanden sind zeitgemäße Interieurs voller Farbenfreude und verspielter Details für Boutique, Eingangshalle, Büros und Modesalons. Die Drapierungen und Dekorationen rufen Erinnerungen an die Eleganz der großen Pariser Modehäuser des 19. Jahrhunderts wach.

In Deutschland gestalteten sie anläßlich der 500-Jahr-Feier des Fürstenhauses von Thurn und Taxis die Innenausstattung des Regensburger Schloßcafés. Hierzu gehörte nicht nur das gesamte Mobiliar und die Beleuchtungskörper, sondern auch das passende Porzellanservice und eine liebevoll gestaltete Besteckserie.

The result were up-to-date interiors: a boutique, lobby, offices and fashion salons that were cheerfully colourful as well as rich in playful detail. The draperies and decorations call to mind the elegance of the grand Parisian fashion houses of the last century.

In Germany, the two designed the interior of the café at Regensburg Castle on the occasion of the 500 anniversary of the Thurn und Taxis royal family. This involved creating not only all the furniture and lighting, but also dreaming up an appropriate coffee service and a lovingly shaped set of cutlery.

Rechts: Ihre "Stilisierung" erfährt diese schlichte Vase erst durch die drei applizierten "Goldfüße". Maße: ø 17 cm, 29,5 cm hoch
Right: The "stylisation" of this simple vase is achieved by means of the three applied "golden feet". ø 17 cm, height: 29.5 cm

WORKSHOP COLOUR COMEDIES

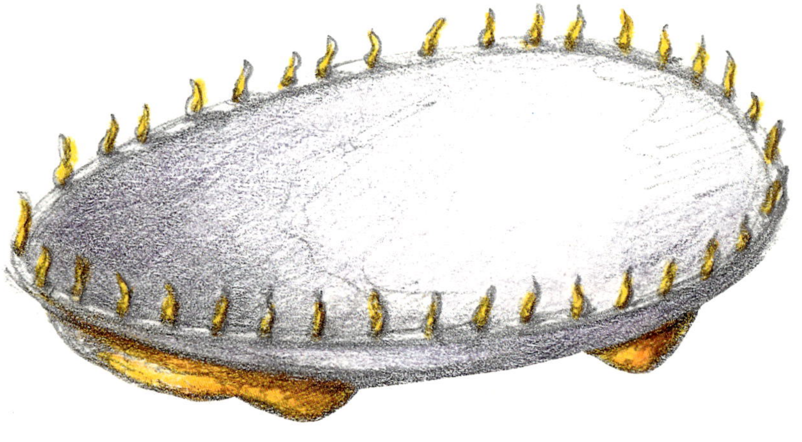

Mit ihren Entwürfen verfolgten die beiden Designer Garouste und Bonetti die Geschichte der Keramik bis zu ihren Ursprüngen zurück. Archaische Formen wurden prunkvoll garniert.
Garouste and Bonetti's designs trace the history of ceramics back to their origin. Archaic forms are decorated lavishly.

Bei den Objekten, die für den "Waechtersbacher" Workshop "Colour Comedies" entstanden sind, tritt ein Thema in den Vordergrund, das in ihren Arbeiten schon lange angelegt ist: die "Natur". Ihr erklärtes Ziel: die "nature sophistiquée", die verfremdete, die überhöhte, die verfeinerte, die nicht mehr "natürliche" Natur. Sie verwendeten Fundstücke, wie Kiesel und Lavagestein, deren Formen in Steingut exakt nachempfunden wurden. So entsteht ein bizarrer und gleichzeitig verschwenderisch prunkvoller Eindruck, bei dem Keramik, Dekoration, Farbe und der Charakter eines Naturgesteins harmonisch miteinander verschmelzen.

The objects which they produced for the Waechtersbacher "Colour Comedies" Workshop foreground a theme that has already existed for some time in their work: "Nature". They expressly aim to achieve a "nature sophistiquée", in other words a nature that is alienated, exaggerated, refined, and thus no longer "natural". Garouste and Bonetti use objects trouvées, such as pebbles and igneous rocks, whose forms are perfectly reproduced in earthenware. They thus give the impression of being both bizarre and simultaneously extravagant and sumptuous – ceramics, decorative elements, the colours and the character of natural stone melting into a harmonious whole.

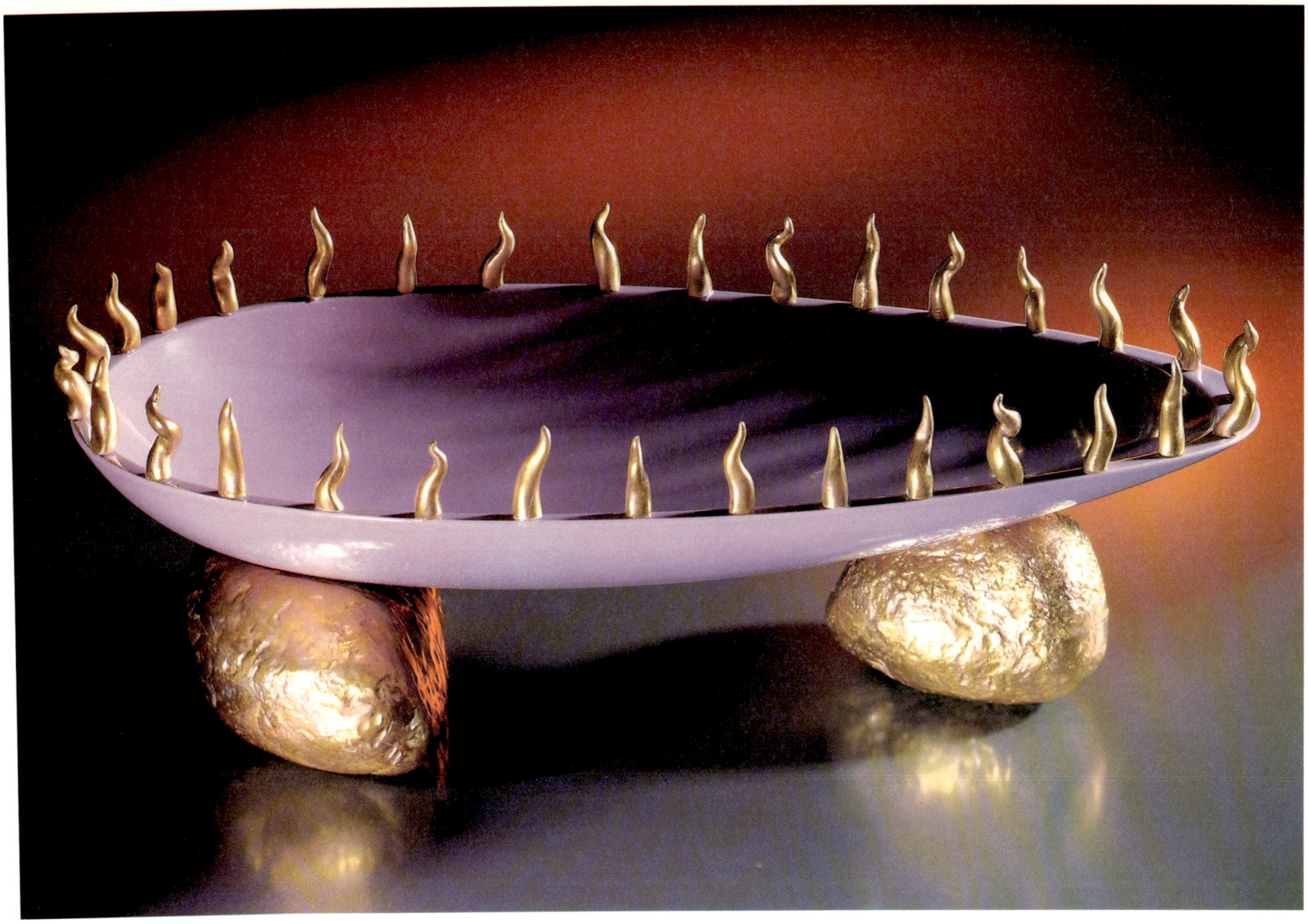

Die applizierten Golddetails, umzüngeln den Schalenrand wie kleine Flammen. Es entsteht der Eindruck von Leichtigkeit und Dynamik.
Maße: 38 cm lang, 32 cm breit, 9,7 cm hoch
The applications in gold, lap round the edge of the bowl like miniature flames. The result is a sense of lightness and movement.
38 cm long, 32 cm wide, 9.7 cm high

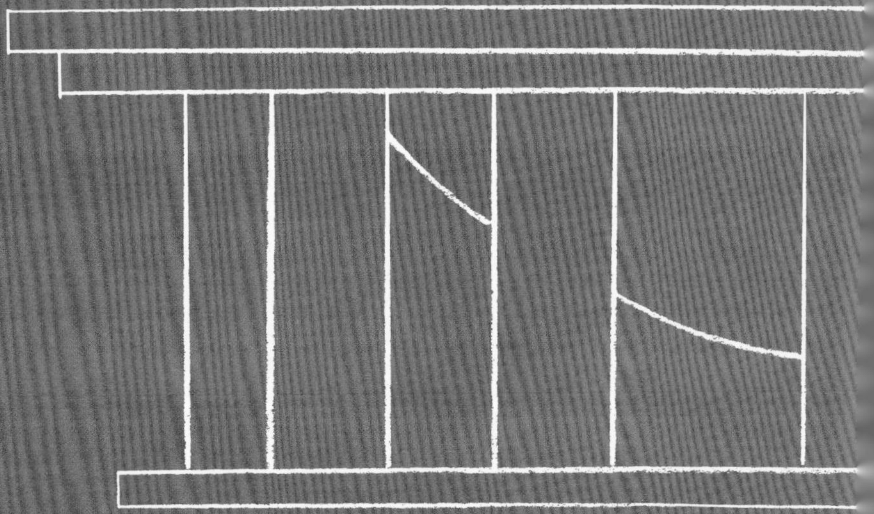

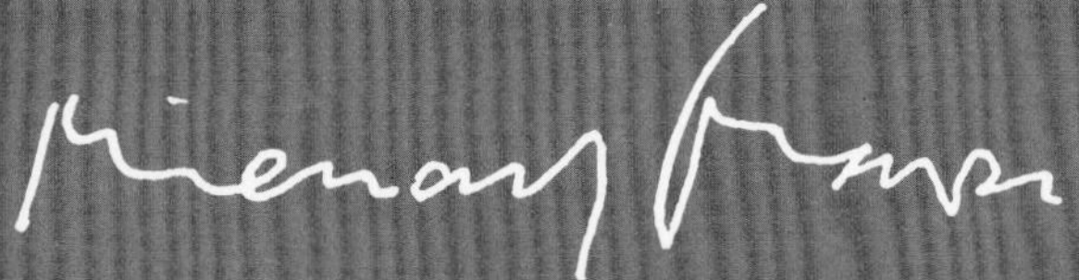

MICHAEL GRAVES

Michael Graves wurde 1934 in Indianapolis geboren. Sein Architekturstudium absolvierte er an der Universität von Cincinnati und an der Harvard Academy. 1960 erhielt er den Rom-Preis, ein Stipendium an der American Academy in Rom, wo er zwei Jahre blieb. Während dieser Zeit entdeckte er, daß Architektur noch andere Möglichkeiten bietet als die klare, abstrakte Formensprache des Funktionalismus. Doch zunächst entwarf er Gebäude, die in der Tradition der Moderne standen.

In den späten 70ern änderte Michael Graves seinen Gestaltungsstil. Er wurde zu einem Protagonisten der "Postmoderne". 1980 gewann er mit einem Entwurf, der Ausdruck dieser neuen Bewegung war, den Wettbewerb für das "Portland Building" in Oregon und entzündete so eine hitzige Debatte in der Architekturszene.

Seine nächsten Triumphe feierte er 1982 mit dem Bau des Humana Buildings und dem gelungenen Um- und Erweiterungsbau für das Newark Museum in Newark, New Jersey. Es folgten zahlreiche Aufträge für repräsentative Gebäude in den Vereinigten Staaten und Japan. 1987 entstanden die Hotelkomplexe "Swan Hotel" und "Dolphin Hotel" in Floridas Walt Disney World.

Michael Graves unterhält derzeit ein Architekturbüro mit 83 Mitarbeitern in Princeton, New Jersey. Dort wird neben Architekturzeichnungen auch an Entwürfen für Möbel, Uhren, Besteck und Porzellan gearbeitet. Der von Michael Graves gestaltete Wasserkessel für die Firma Alessi ist zum Symbol für die Designbegeisterung der 80er Jahre geworden.

Michael Graves was born in Indianapolis in 1934. He studied architecture at the University of Cincinnati and at the Harvard Academy. In 1960 he was awarded the Rome Prize, a scholarship to attend the American Academy in Rome, where he remained for two years. During this time he discovered that there was more to architecture than just the opportunities afforded by the clear abstract forms of functionalism. Yet he nevertheless initially designed buildings in the Modernist tradition.

Graves adopted a radically new style in the late 1970s, becoming one of the leading figures of "Post-Modernism". In 1980 it was his design, an embodiment of this new movement, that was adopted by the competition jury as the basis for the Portland Building in Oregon, sparking off a heated debate in the architectural world.

His next triumphs were not long in coming: in 1982 he designed the Humana Building in Louisville, Kentucky and was in charge of the restructuring work and the design of the new wing of the Newark Museum in New Jersey. Numerous contracts followed to create representative edifices in the United States and Japan. And in 1987, the two major Swan Hotel and Dolphin Hotel complexes in Florida's Walt Disney World were both completed.

Michael Graves currently runs at Princeton, New Jersey an architectural office that employs 83 staff members. Not only does the studio output include architectural blueprints, but also designs for furniture, watches, cutlery and porcelain. Michael Graves draft for a kettle for the Alessi company became a symbol of the 1980s enthusiasm for design.

Das Swan Hotel auf dem Gelände der Walt Disney World in Florida, 1987.
The Swan Hotel on the grounds of Disney World in Florida, 1987.

Michael Graves gilt als eine der Zentralfiguren der Postmoderne. Er hat sie mitentwickelt und mit seinen zunächst umstrittenen Entwürfen die öffentliche Diskussion bestimmt und vorangetrieben.

Schon 1982 schreibt Paul Goldberger im New York Times Magazin: "Wenn Philip Johnson als eine Art Pate der Postmoderne verstanden wird, so ist Michael Graves zumindest in den Augen der Öffentlichkeit ihre Verkörperung geworden."[2]

Er verlieh der Postmoderne ihr Gesicht nicht nur auf dem Gebiet der Architektur, er gestaltete einfach jede denkbare Spielart des Konsumgutes. Es entstand eine ganze Palette an Stühlen, Tischen, Lampen, Stoff- und Teppichdessins, Uhren, Porzellan, Bestecken bis hin zur Tragetasche.

Noch in den 60er Jahren beschäftige Graves sich ausgiebig mit dem Funktionalismus. Klare, strenge Formen dominierten seine Architektur.

Mit dem Einsatz klarer, leuchtender Farben und einfallsreicher Details begann er sich langsam von seinen Vorbildern der klassischen Moderne zu lösen. Ende der 70er Jahre verwarf er seine bisher geleistete Arbeit.

Er erkannte, daß sich die funktionalistische Architektur an den Bedürfnissen der Menschen vorbeientwickelt hatte. "Die Moderne Architektur war so abstrakt, daß der Mann auf der Straße eine Art Text brauchte, um zu verstehen, was vor sich ging."[3] Er wollte zu einer Architektur finden, die wieder verstanden werden konnte.

Seine Stilmittel, um dieses Ansinnen zu verwirklichen, fand er, wie andere postmoderne Architekten, in der klassischen Architektur und in den sich daran anlehnenden Stilrichtungen der Renaissance und des Klassizismus. Er verwendete Säulen als dekorative Elemente seiner Architektur. Erker wurden in die Fassaden eingeschoben und verspielte Details appliziert.

Der starke Einsatz von Farbe hat sich zu einem Charakteristikum Gravescher Architektur entwickelt. Er hat sich ein eigenes Farbspektrum entwickelt, das er niemals verläßt. Es handelt sich um warme Farben, Erdtöne wie Ocker oder Terracotta, die mit einem gebrochenen, blassen Blau oder Grün kombiniert werden. Diese Farben, die als "Graves-Töne" gelten, transportieren hervorragend seinen klassischen, eklektischen Anspruch. Wirken sie doch wie von der Palette eines Renaissance-Malers entnommen.

Pastellzeichnung von Michael Graves für das Swan Hotel.
Chalk pastel draft of the Swan Hotel by Michael Graves.

Oben: Archaische Gefäße, hergestellt von der Firma Steuben.
Darunter: Sanders Dining Room mit dem Tafelservice "Delos", 1987.
Top: Archaic glass vessels, manufactured by the Steuben company.
Bottom: Sanders Dining Room with the "Delos" dinner service, 1987.

Michael Graves can be considered one of the central figures of post-modernism. He has been part responsible for the form that movement has taken and has both guided and caused much public discussion with his initially controversial designs.

As early as 1982, Paul Goldberger wrote in the New York Times Magazine that "if Philip Johnson stands as a kind of godfather to postmodernism, Michael Graves has now become, in the public eye at least, its very embodiment[2]."

He not only shaped the face of post-modernism in the field of architecture but has also simply designed all conceivably types of consumer goods. The result has been a massive range of chairs, tables, lamps, fabric and carpet designs, watches, porcelain, cutlery and even carrier bags.

The 1960s found Graves still intensively studying functionalism. His architecture was characterized by clear, strict forms. He started to cut the umbilical cord to his classic Modernist models with the gradual introduction of clear, bright colours and imaginative details. At the end of the 1970s he rejected all his past work and recognized that functionalist architecture had developed further without taking the actual human needs into account. "Modern architecture was so abstract that the man on the street needed a kind of text to understand what went on[3]." He wished to hit upon a form of architecture that people could understand once more.

He came across the stylistic means to achieve this end, as did other post-modern architects, in classical architecture and in Renaissance and Classicist styles that took the latter up. He utilized columns as decorative elements in his drafts, bay windows were inset into the facades and playful details added.

The strong use of colour evolved as a standard feature of Graves architecture, and he devised his own spectrum of colours which he has used ever since. He opts for warm colours, earthly hues such as ocre or terracotta, which can be combined in relation to a broken and pale blue or green. These colours, which are meanwhile considered "Graves tones", function as exceptional vehicles for his classical, eclectic project, for the effect they have is similar to that achieved by hues taken from the palette of a Renaissance painter.

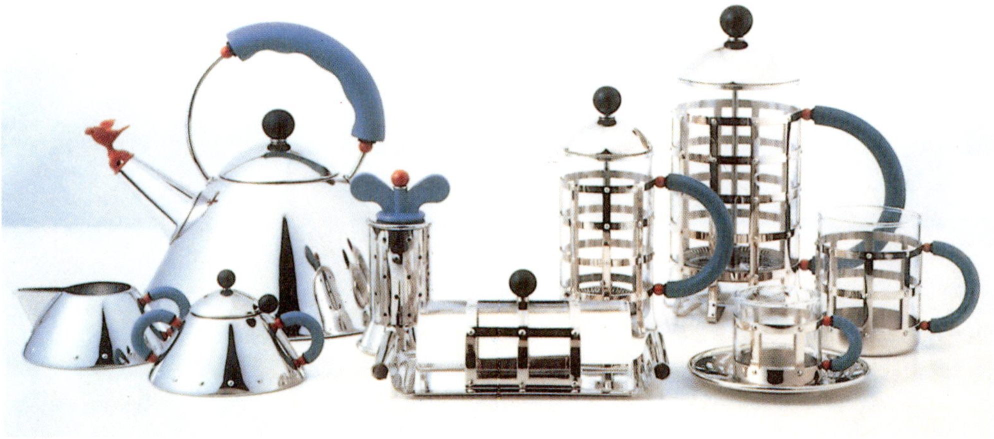

Produktfamilie. Diese Entwürfe für die Firma Alessi machten Graves als Designer weltberühmt, 1985-1990.
Designs for a product family for Alessi which made Graves world famous as a designer, 1985-1990.

WORKSHOP COLOUR COMEDIES

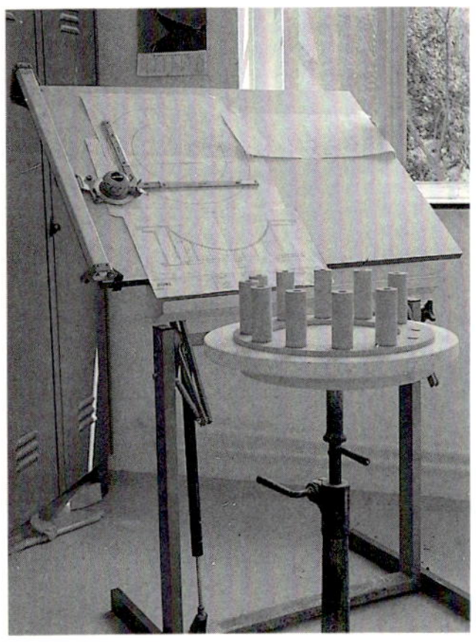

Für den Workshop "Colour Comedies" entwickelte Michael Graves eine Obstschale. "Ich wollte ein Gefäß entwickeln," kommentiert Michael Graves, "das sowohl zeitgemäß sei, als auch etwas jener klassischen Langlebigkeit an sich haben würde, mittels derer es sich vieleicht über einen längeren Zeitraum bewähren könnte. Für die Obstschale nahm ich satte Farben, da sie sich stark von dem darauf liegenden Obst absetzen sollten. Ich dachte, es sei spannender, ein Objekt herzustellen, das sowohl pragmatisch als auch künstlerisch orientiert ist, und nicht nur eines von beiden. Ich habe mich immer für Gefäße interessiert und besitze eine kleine Sammlung von griechischen, etruskischen und römischen Töpfen und sogar einige aus den Wiener Werkstätten."

For the "Colour Comedies" Workshop, Michael Graves dreamed up a fruit bowl. "I wanted to design a vessel," he himself says, "that was both interesting to the modern eye and also have a more classical longevity so that it could, perhaps, stand the test of time. I used rich colors for this fruit bowl because I wanted the vessel to stand in strong contrast to the fruit is ment to hold. I thought it more interesting to make an object that was both pragmatic and artistic and not simply the one or the other. I have always been interested in vessels, in fact, I have a small collection of Greek, Etruscan and Roman pots as well as vessels from the Vienna Werkstätten."

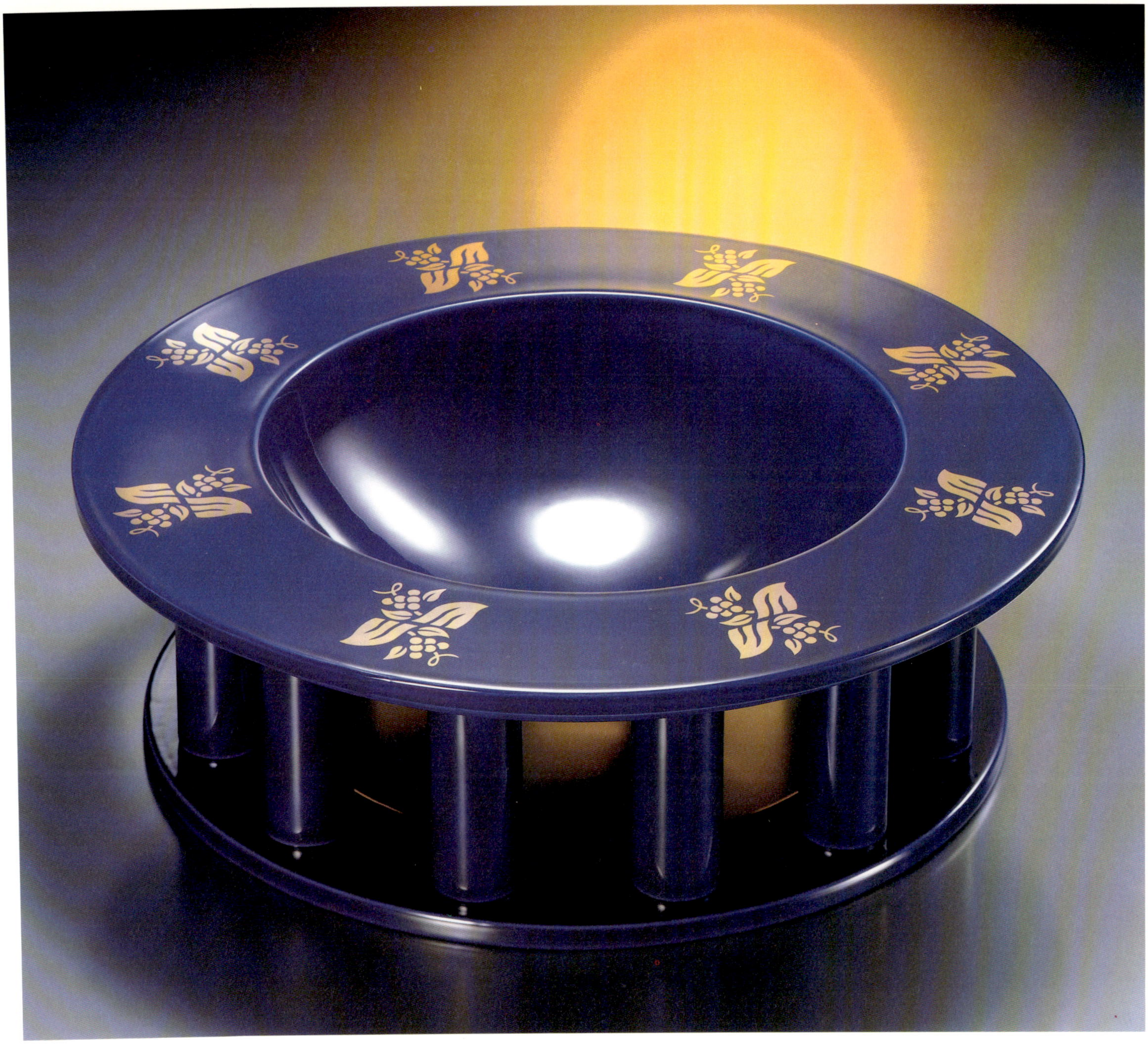

"Ich dachte, es sei spannender, ein Objekt herzustellen, das sowohl pragmatisch als auch künstlerisch orientiert ist, und nicht nur eines von beiden." (Michael Graves)
Maße: ø 44,5 cm, 13,2 cm hoch

"I thought it more interesting to make an object that was both pragmatic and artistic and not simply the one or the other." (Michael Graves)
ø 44.5 cm,13.2 cm high

ZAHA HADID

Zaha Hadid wurde 1950 in Bagdad geboren. In Beirut studierte sie an der Amerikanischen Universität Mathematik und machte 1971 ihren Abschluß. Danach ging sie nach London und studierte Architektur an der Architectural Association School, die sie 1977 mit Auszeichnung abschloß und an der sie bis 1987 auch unterrichtete.

Mit ihren architekonischen Entwürfen, die dem "Dekonstruktivismus" verpflichtet sind, wurde sie schnell international bekannt.
In der Zeit zwischen 1986 und 87 hatte Zaha Hadid Gastprofessuren an den Universitäten von Harvard und Columbia. Immer wieder wird sie zu Vorträgen und Konferenzen in Europa und den Vereinigten Staaten eingeladen.

1982 erhielt sie die Gold Medaille für ihren Entwurf zum Umbau einer luxuriösen Maisonette-Wohnung am Eaton Place in London. Den nächsten Wettbewerb gewann sie ein Jahr später mit ihren Plänen zur Errichtung des Freizeitparks "The Peak Club" in Hongkong. Sie wurde zur Internationalen Bauausstellung in Berlin eingeladen und gewann den Wettbewerb für ein Gebäude am Kurfürstendamm in Berlin. 1989 setzte sie sich in dem Wettbewerb zum "Mediapark" in Düsseldorf durch.
1986-88 entwickelte sie verschiedene Sitzmöbel für die Firma Edra. Es entstanden Dessins für Teppichböden der Firma Vorwerk und ein Porzellanservice, das von Swid Powell produziert wurde.

Ihre Arbeiten wurden schon 1978 im Guggenheim-Museum ausgestellt. Es folgte 1985 eine Ausstellung in der GA Gallerie in Tokio. 1988 nahm sie an der von Philip Johnson und Mark Wigley organisierten Ausstellung "Deconstructiviste Architecture" teil.

Zaha Hadid was born in Baghdad in 1950. She studied mathematics at the American University in Beirut, graduating in 1971. She then left for London, where she studied architecture at the Architectural Association School, from where she graduated with a distinction for excellence in 1977.

She soon became known internationally for her architectonic designs, which are fully imbued with the spirit of deconstructivism.

From 1986-87, Zaha Hadid was visiting professor at both Harvard and Columbia universities. She has repeatedly been invited to lecture or to attend conferences in Europe and the United States.

In 1982 she received the gold medal for her draft for the redesigning of a luxury maisonette in Eaton Place, London. She won a further competition the following year, this time with plans for the creation of "The Peak Club" leisure park in Hong Kong. She was invited to attend the International Construction Exhibition in Berlin, and promptly won the competition to design a building for the Kurfürstendamm in Berlin. In 1989 it was her project that won the day for the new "Media Park" in Düsseldorf.

Between 1986 and 1988 she developed various forms of seating for the Edra company, not to mention carpeting designs for Vorwerk and tableware that was then manufactured by Swid Powell.

Her work was displayed at the Guggenheim Museum as early as 1978, to be followed by an exhibition at the GA Gallery in Tokyo in 1985. In 1988 she contributed to "Deconstructiviste Architecture"; a show mounted by Philip Johnson and Mark Wigley.

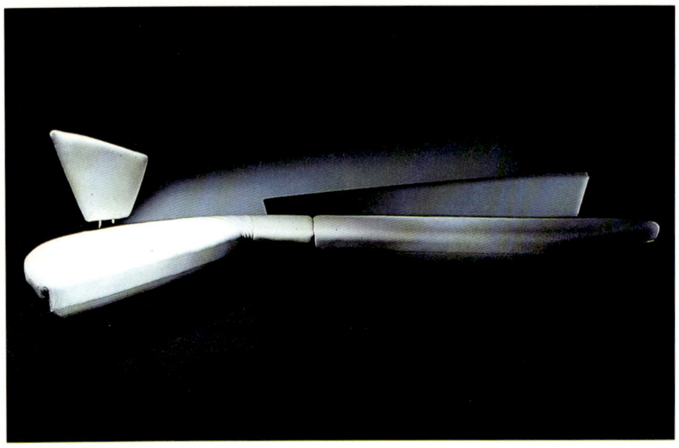

Die irakische Architektin Zaha M. Hadid wird mit ihrer Architektur dem "Dekonstruktivismus" zugerechnet. Einem Stil, der in den 80er Jahren international bekannt geworden ist. Merkmal dieser neuen Richtung in der Architektur ist die Zergliederung und das Aufbrechen von normalerweise geschlossenen Raumstrukturen. Inspirationen für ihre Arbeit fanden die Architekten dieses neuen Stils in der russischen Revolutionsarchitektur.

Auch Zaha Hadid trägt den Werten und Visionen der "Russischen Avantgarde" Rechnung, ohne den romantischen Anspruch, durch ihre Entwürfe zu einer besseren Weltordnung beizutragen zu wollen, wie es ihre "Mentoren", die Architekten des "Konstruktivismus" noch beabsichtigten. Sie verwendet vielmehr die radikalen Maximen der konstruktivistischen Architekten,um einen Beitrag zu unserer modernen Kultur und zur Erneuerung unserer Städte zu leisten.

Sofa "Wavy Back", 1987-1988 und "Whoosh" Sofa 1986-1987. Edra Spa., Perignano, Italien.
"Wavy Back" sofa, 1987-88 and "Whoosh" sofa, 1986-87. Manufactured by Edra Spa., Perignano, Italy.

Sofa "Red Projection", 1987-88 für Edra.
Sofa "Red Projection", 1987-88 for Edra.

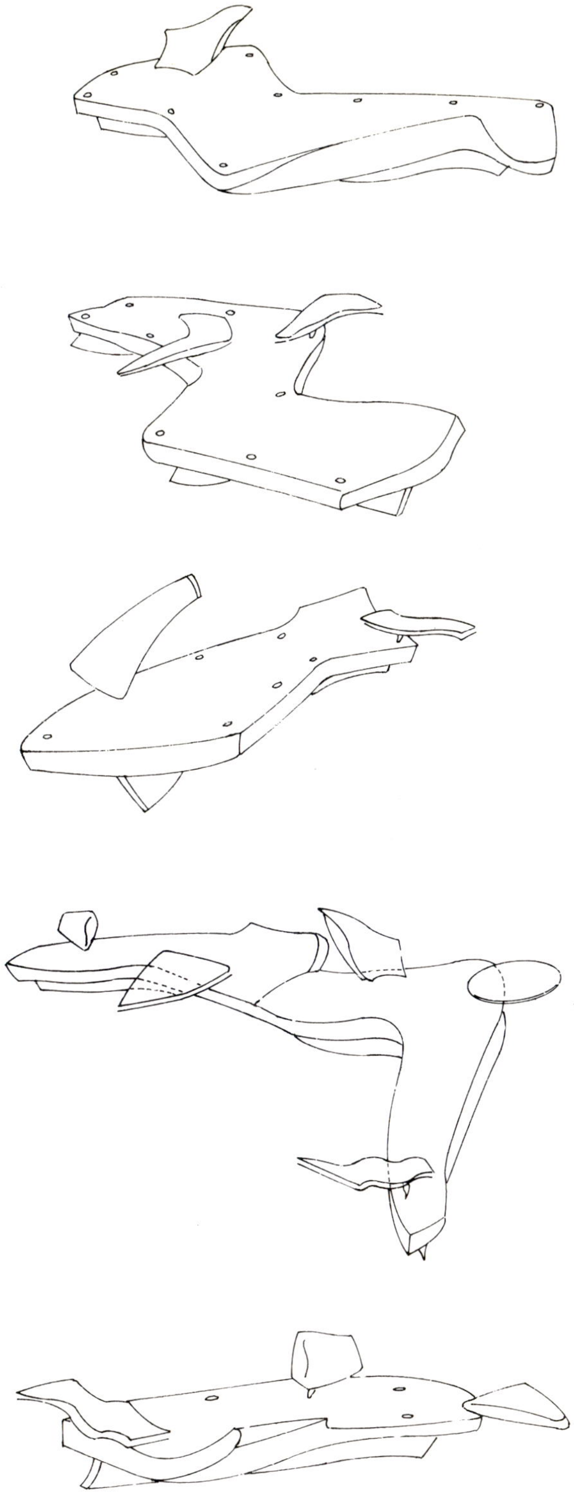

Iraqi architect Zaha Hadid is generally classified, together with her architecture, which is strongly indebted to deconstructivism alongside the deconstructivists, whose style came to international prominence in the 1980s. Characteristic of this new current in architecture was its tendency to dissect and break open room structures that are normally closed.

Deconstructivist architects sought and found inspiration for their work in the architecture of the Russian Revolution. Like them, Zaha Hadid also takes the values and visions of the "Russian avantgarde" into account, yet makes no attempt – as her "mentors", the architect of constructivism, still did – to fulfil some romantic claim to contribute with her plans to the creation of a better world. Rather, she makes use of the radical maxims of constructivist architecture in order to play a part in augmenting our modern culture or revitalizing our cities.

Die Bar im ersten Stock des "Moonsoon" Restaurants in Sapporo, Japan.
The bar on the first floor of the "Moonsoon" Restaurant in Sapporo, Japan.

Entwürfe für Sitzmöbel, die 1987 für das Restaurant "Moonsoon" in Sapporo, Japan, entstanden.
Designs for seating furniture, commissioned in 1987 for the "Moonsoon"Restaurant in Sapporo, Japan.

WORKSHOP COLOUR COMEDIES

Bisher hat Zaha Hadid ihren großen Einfluß auf das internationale Architekturgeschehen vor allem durch ihre Architekturzeichnungen und Gemälde ausgeübt. Ihren kühnen und einzigartigen Zeichenstil entwickelte sie in der Auseinandersetzung mit Malewitsch und der von ihm entwickelten Kunstform des Suprematismus. Malewitsch verfolgte mit seinen abstrakten Bildern das Ziel, ein neues Raumgefühl zu vermitteln und die "reine Emotion" zu thematisieren. Durch die Beschäftigung mit dem Suprematismus erfuhr sie, daß der Plan mehr sein mußte als eine bloße Konstruktionszeichnung. Durch Malewitsch erkannte sie, "daß es noch eine andere Kraft gibt, daß man frei von bestimmten Restriktionen"[4] und der "existierenden Ordnung"[5] arbeiten muß. Es sind gerade diese Einflüsse, die sie in ihrer Arbeit verfolgt und zu einer eigenen Architektursprache entwickelt hat. Das führt zu der atemberaubenden Wirkung ihrer Entwürfe, die sich von der herrschenden Schwerkraft zu lösen scheinen, und damit den Eindruck von frei durch den Raum schwebenden Objekten vermitteln.

To date, it has been Zaha Hadid's architectural drawings and paintings that have had the greatest impact on international architecture. She developed her daring and unique style of drawing through a critical study of Malevich and suprematism, the art movement he called into being. Malevich's goal was, by means of his abstract pictures, to convey a new feeling of space and to stress "pure emotion" as a theme. Hadid's study of suprematism kindled her conviction that an architectural plan had to be more than a mere drawing outlining the construction of a building. Instead, a plan had to become an instrument that opened the door looking out onto her own personal architectonic visions. And it was by studying Malevich that she realized that "there is another force that you are free from a certain restriction"[4] and "the existing orders."[5] It is precisely these influences which she endeavours to elaborate in her work, giving rise to an architectural language of her own. And it is precisely this which underlies the breathtaking effect of her plans, which seem to be liberated from the sway of gravity and convey an impression of their being objects that float freely in space.

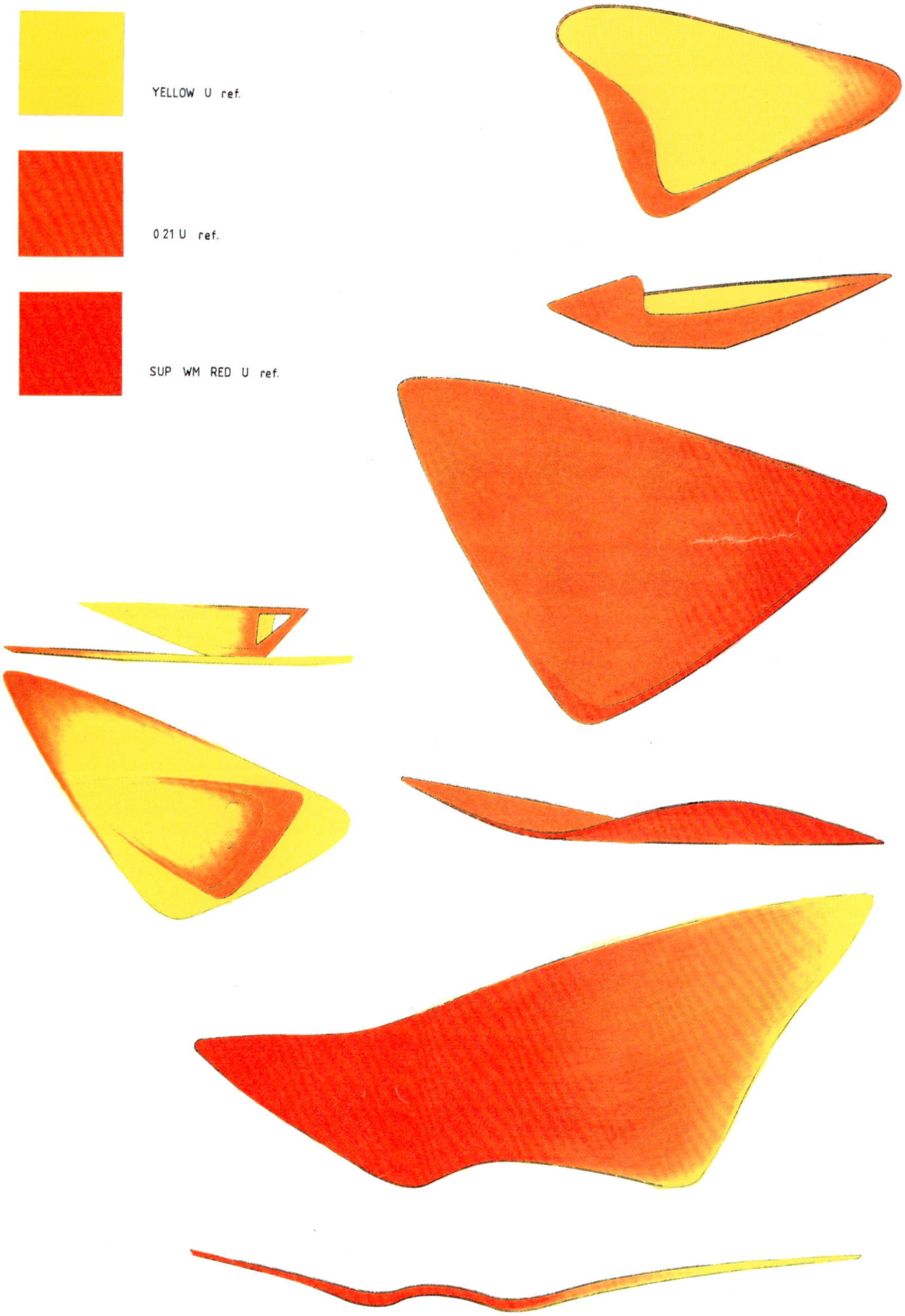

Farbskizze für den Workshop "Colour Comedies". Die Produktfamilie "chips" stellt eine Reihe von Variationen zu dem Thema "Feuer" dar.
Colour sketch for the "Colour Comedies" Workshop. The "chips" product family constitutes a series of variations on the theme of "fire".

Mit dieser Technik ist es ihr gelungen, unter 600 Bewerbungen für den Wettbewerb um den Freizeitclub "The Peak Club" in Hongkong als Siegerin hervorzutreten. Spätestens durch diesen Erfolg hat sie internationales Profil gewonnen und wurde zu einer der Protagonisten des "Dekonstruktivismus". Doch sind bisher erst wenige Ideen von Zaha Hadid realisiert worden. Die italienische Firma Edra hat einige farbenfrohe und elegante Sofa-Modelle umgesetzt. Ein innenarchitektonischer Entwurf wurde in Japan verwirklicht. Im "Moonsoon" Restaurant in Sapporo wird das für Zaha Hadid typische Thema "Energie" behandelt. "Feuer" und "Eis" stehen sich als Gegenspieler für die beiden Bereiche Restaurant und Bar gegenüber.

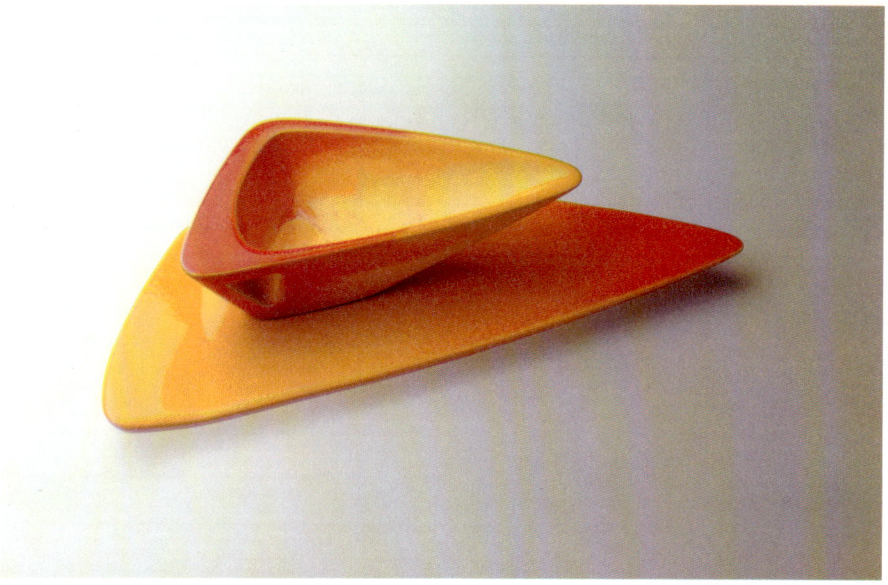

Frei von einer "existierenden Ordnung" arbeitet Zaha Hadid. Auch einem Alltagsobjekt wie einer Tasse verleiht sie die typische spitze, dreieckige Form.

Zaha Hadid's work is not constrained by any "existing order". Even such a mundane object as a cup receives a typically pointed, triangular form in her hands.

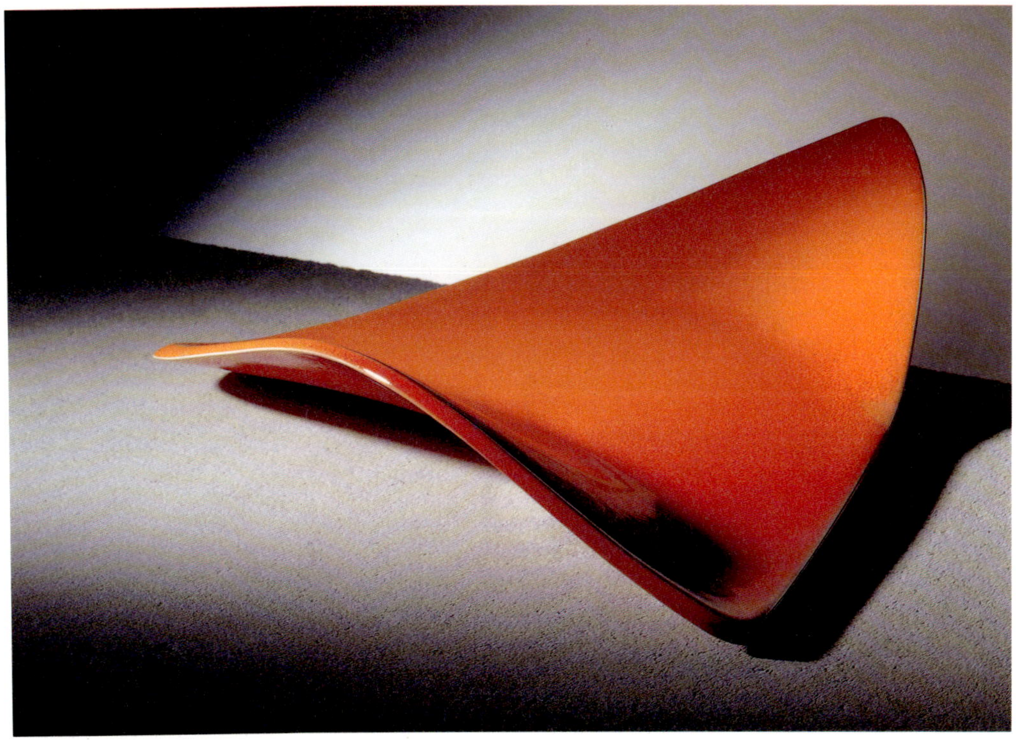

Elegant wölbt sich diese Schale in den Raum. Auch bei diesem Objekt haben die Fachkräfte der Waechtersbacher Keramik gezeigt, daß sie ihr Handwerk perfekt beherrschen. Dem in seiner ursprünglichen Form weichen tonkeramischen Material einen so kühnen und gleichmäßigen Schwung zu geben, ist eine Leistung, die erwähnt werden muß.
Maße: 43,5 cm lang, 34 cm breit, 5,7 cm hoch

This bowl extends in an elegant wavy line across space. Here again the craftsmen and -women at Waechtersbacher Keramik have had the chance to prove the degree to which they have perfected their skills. Giving such a bold and uniform line to such a soft material as the original ceramic clay is a feat that should not go unmentioned.
43.5cm long, 34 cm wide, 5.7 cm high

It was this approach which gave her submission the edge over the other 600 odd entries to the competition for a design for the Hong Kong "Peak Club" leisure facility. At the latest since this success her work has gained a truly international stature and she has become one of the leading figures of deconstructivism. Yet to date only a very few of her ideas have been implemented. The Italian Edra company has produced some highly colourful and elegant examples of Hadid furniture. One interior design project in Japan has been realized: the Sapporo "Moonsoon" Restaurant now sports an interior which focuses on "energy", a topic typical of Zaha Hadid's work. "Fire" and "ice" confront one another as opponents, representing the restaurant and the bar respectively.

Ein Entwurf aus der Serie "chips". Großzügig durchmißt die splitterförmige Schale den Raum, nur an zwei Punkten berührt sie die darunter sich ausbreitende Fläche . Die für Zaha Hadid typische Illusion des "Schwebens" wird von der Zeichnung auf das realisierte Produkt übertragen. Hier scheinen die Gesetze der Schwerkraft und der Steingutproduktion gleichermaßen aufgehoben zu sein. Den Fachkräften der Waechtersbacher Keramik ist das handwerkliche Kunststück gelungen, mit dem ja zunächst weichen tonkeramischen Material eine steil ansteigende und vollkommen ungestützte Fläche zu erzeugen.
Maße: 60 cm lang, 21,9 cm breit, 4,5 cm hoch

A draft from the "chips"line. The splinter-shaped bowl stretches out suspended in space, only touching the surface beneath it at two points. The illusion of "floating" typical of Zaha Hadid's work is then transformed from the status of a drawing into a real product. Here, Hadid seems to be defying not only the laws of gravity but also the laws of ceramics production. The skilled craftsmen and -women at Waechtersbacher Keramik had to pull off a minor miracle of workmanship in order to create a sharply inclining yet completely unsupported surface fromthe initially pliable ceramic clay material.
60 cm long, 21.9 cm wide, 4.5 cm high

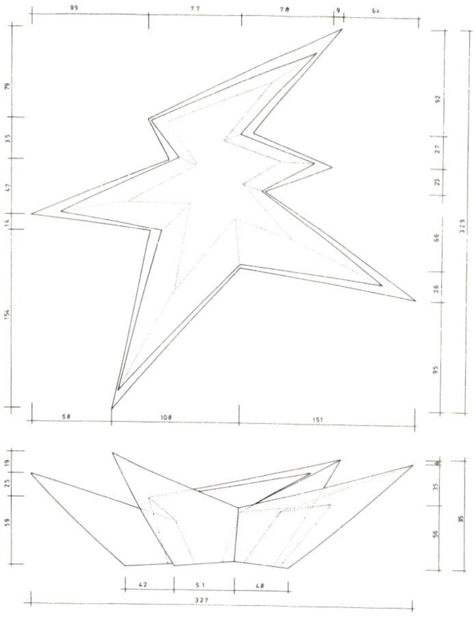

Architektonische Formen werden von Zaha Haid bei dieser Schale wieder aufgenommen.
Zaha Hadid takes up architectonic forms in designing this bowl.

Der Themenbereich "Energie" ist zu einem zentralen Moment ihrer Entwurfstätigkeit geworden. Für den Workshop "Colour Comedies" entwarf sie eine sternenförmige, violette Schale und die Produktfamilie "chips", was soviel wie "Splitter" bedeutet. Die Objekte der "chips"-Familie haben eine kräftigen, orange-roten Farbverlauf, der gemeinsam mit den spitzen Formen erneut das Thema "Feuer" aufnimmt.

"Energy" as a topic has become a central strand in Hadid's thought as a designer. For the "Colour Comedies" Workshop she designed a star-shaped violet bowl and the "chips" product family, chips meaning fragments here. The objects "chips" are a blend of oranges and reds taking up the theme of "fire" already suggested by their jagged flame-like forms.

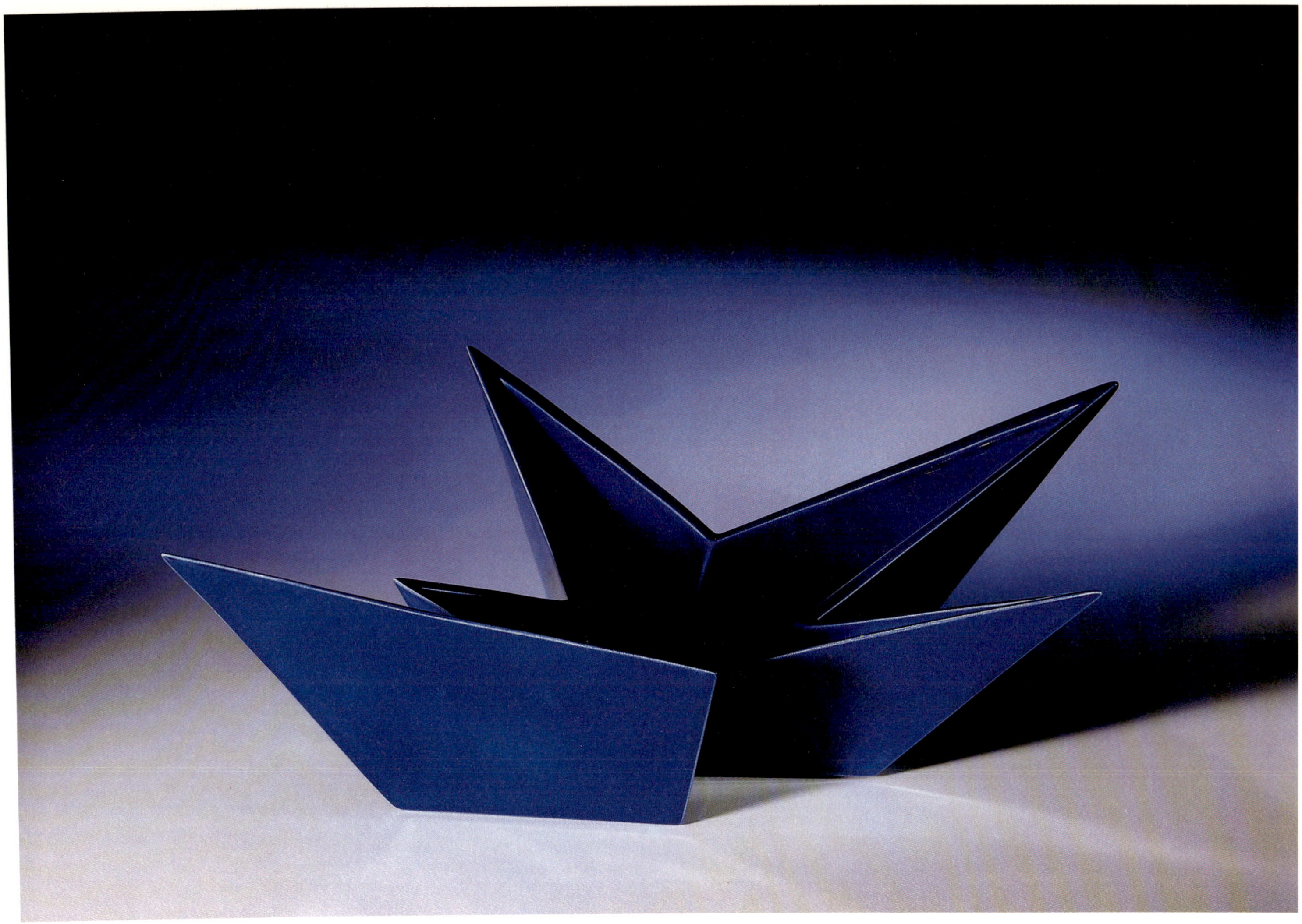

Der Themenbereich "Energie" ist zu einem zentralen Moment ihrer Entwurfstätigkeit geworden. Unruhig gruppieren sich die spitzen Strahlen um den Mittelpunkt der Schale.

"Energy" as a topic has become a central strand in Hadid's thought as a designer. The pointed, ray-like ends of the bowl are grouped restlessly around its centre.

Atsushi Kitagawara

ATSUSHI KITAGAWARA

Atsushi Kitagawara wurde 1951 in Tokio geboren. 1971 erwarb er sein Diplom als Architekt an der University of Fine Arts in Tokio, an der er seit 1991 auch unterrichtet.

Die Gebäude und Möbel von Atsushi Kitagawara stellen eine persönliche Interpretation literarischer Werke dar. Schriftsteller wie André Breton, Philippe Soupault, Antonin Artaud und Franz Kafka haben ihn zu seinen Architektur- und Materialcollagen inspiriert.

Schon 1980 gründete er sein eigenes Architekturstudio, "Kitagawara ILCD Architects". Noch im gleichen Jahr baute er in Tokio das "Miaon-kaku", einen Gebäudekomplex bestehend aus der verblüffenden Kombination von Büroeinrichtungen und heiliger Stätte. 1986 entstand der Kinokomplex "Cinema Rise" in Tokio, eine gewagte, aber gekonnte Architekturcollage, die ihn auch über die Grenzen Japans hinaus bekannt gemacht hat. 1987 wurde das Bürogebäude "Minato Ward" fertig gestellt. Es folgten 1989 das "Edoken Tokio Head Office" und 1991 das "Santo Industry Head Office".

Atsushi Kitagawara was born in Tokyo in 1951. In 1971 he gained his degree in architecture from Tokyo University of Fine Arts, where he has been a lecturer since 1991.

Kitagawara's buildings and furniture are the designer's personal interpretation of literary works. Writers such as André Breton, Philippe Soupault, Antonin Artaud and Franz Kafka have provided the inspiration for his architectural and material collages.

By 1980 he had already founded his own architectural studio, "Kitagawara ILCD Architects". That same year he built the "Miaon-kaku" complex in Tokyo, a remarkable combination which is part office building, part place of religion. 1986 saw the construction of his "Cinema Rise" movie theatre centre, a daring but masterly architectural collage which spread his fame beyond the shores of Japan. The "Minato Ward office building" was completed in 1987, followed in 1989 by the "Edoken Tokyo Head Office" and in 1991 by the "Santo Industry Head Office".

"Haus 395". 1986 entwarf Atsushi Kitagawara dieses Gebäude, in dem er heute sein Studio eingerichtet hat.
"House 395". Atsushi Kitagawara designed this building in 1986, and today it houses his studio.

Atsushi Kitagawara ist ein Architekt der Metropole. Die Großstadt mit ihrer verworrenen Technologie, ihren mannigfaltigen Informationsprozessen und ökonomischen Mechanismen fasziniert ihn und ist der Nährboden für seine Architektur. Seine Heimatstadt Tokio sieht er als wichtigen Impulsgeber für seine Arbeit. "Meine Gebäude sind genau wie der Charakter japanischer Städte, – wie die Düsternis von Tokio."[6]

Seine Möbel und seine Architektur zeichnen sich durch bizarre, zergliederte, ja man könnte meinen, "dekonstruktivistische" Formen aus. Aber von "Dekonstruktivismus" als Referenz für seine Ideen möchte er nichts wissen. Seine Bezüge sieht er vielmehr außerhalb der Architektur.

"Es ist ein einsames Unterfangen, die Architektur zu bereinigen, um sie als eigenständige Disziplin zu etablieren. Meine Anstrengungen gehen weg von einer Architektur funktioneller Betrachtungsweise und hin zu einer poetischen Form des Schaffens. Mein Blickwinkel auf den architektonischen Schöpfungsprozeß ist anders. Ich betrachte die Architektur nur als eine Aktivität unter ganz vielen anderen gesellschaftlichen Aktivitäten, wie beispielsweise Wirtschaft, Kultur und Politik, oder auch persönliche Entwicklungen in meinem eigenen Leben."[7]

"Oda Haus". Wohnhaus, 1990.
"Oda House". a residential dwelling, 1990.

"Verdi" Regal, entworfen 1988 für Tendo-Mokko.
"Verdi" shelf, designed in 1988 for Tendo-Mokko.

Atsushi Kitagawara is a truly metropolitan architect. The city, with its confusing mass of technology, its numerous forms of communication and its economic mechanisms is something that fascinates him and is the lifeblood of his architecture. He regards his home city of Tokyo as providing an important stimulus to his work: "My buildings perfectly resemble the character of Japanese cities – like the gloominess of Tokyo."[6]

The main features of his furniture and his buildings are bizarre, dissected, indeed one could even say "deconstructivist" forms. Yet he utterly rejects any mention of "deconstructivism" as a reference point for his ideas. He prefers to take his points of reference from outside architecture.

"Purifying architecture to establish its independence is a lonely business. What I am trying to do is make the jump from functional to poetic references for architecture. I have a different perspective on the process of producing architecture. Considering architecture as just one of the spheres of social activity in the whole range – from economics, culture, politics, to events in my own personal life – ensures that it is a cross-section of a thought coincidentally cut off at a given point."[7]

"Daphodil" Sofa, entworfen 1988 für Tendo-Mokko.
"Daphodil" sofa, designed in 1988 for Tendo-Mokko.

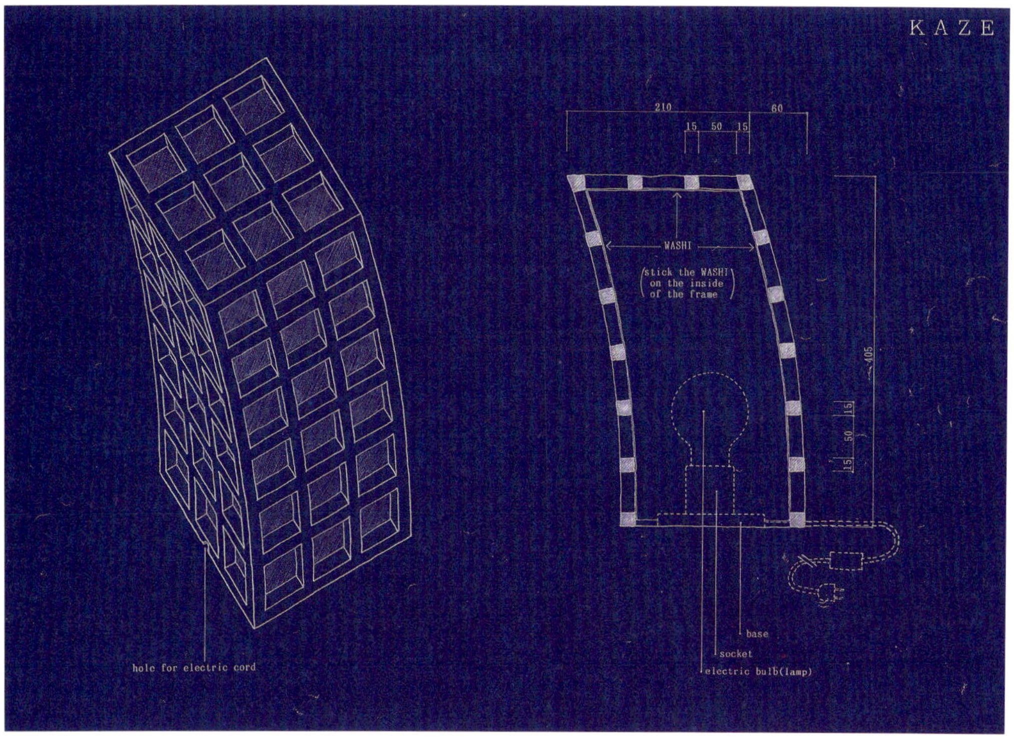

Für den Workshop "Colour Comedies" entwarf Atsushi Kitagawara eine Lampe. Der Lampenkorpus wurde aus Steingut gefertigt und mit Japanpapier"Washi" hinterlegt. Hier nimmt er ganz stark Bezug zur traditionellen Ästhetik und Lebensphilosophie Japans. "Das Zusammentreffen und die Harmonie des harten Materials Keramik mit "Washi" geben einer schlichten Form eine komplexe Spannung und ein wunderschönes Ungleichgewicht", erklärt Atsushi Kitagawara zu seinem Entwurf. In der japanischen Ästhetik wird Harmonie und Vollendung in der Unausgewogenheit gesucht.

"Kaze" nennt er seine Lampe, dies bedeutet auf japanisch "Wind". Der Wind ist eines der wichtigsten, traditionell japanischen Elemente. Wind, Boden, Wasser und Feuer bilden gemeinsam die Welt. Die Leuchte "Kaze" ist ein japanischer Lampion, der dem Wind trotzt und vom ihm verformt wird.

Skizze zur Lampe "Kaze" von Atsushi Kitagawara.
Sketch for Kitagawara's "Kaze" lamp.

Das Erstellen eines solchen filigranen Gerüsts aus Steingut stellte größte Ansprüche an die Handwerkskunst der Formenbauer.
Making such a delicate stoneware framework demands utmost craftsmanship on the part of the mould constructors.

Atsushi Kitagawara designed a lamp for the "Colour Comedies" Workshop. The body of the lamp is made of stoneware and lined with Japanese "Washi" paper attached to the ceramic on the inside. Here Kitagawara refers very clearly to traditional Japanese aesthetics and that culture's philosophy of life. He explains the design by saying that "the encounter and harmony of hard ceramic material with 'Washi' creates complex tension and a beautiful disequilibrium in what is otherwise a simple form." According to Japanese aesthetics, it is in disequilibrium that harmony and perfection are to be found.

He calls his lamp "Kaze", which, as Kitagawara himself explains means "wind" in Japanese, traditionally one of the most important of the elements in Japanese culture. Wind, earth, water and fire go together to form our world. "Kaze" is a Japanese lantern, which defies the wind and is deformed by it.

In der japanischen Ästhetik wird Harmonie und Vollendung in der Unausgewogenheit gesucht. Die Lampe "Kaze", zu deutsch "Wind", bleibt dieser Tradition treu.
Maße: 20,5 cm lang, 20,5 cm breit, 39 cm hoch.
According to Japanese aesthetics, it is in disequilibrium that harmony and perfection are to be found. The "Kaze" lamp, meaning "Wind", is true to this tradition.
20.5 cm long, 20.5 cm wide and 39 cm high.

JO LAUBNER

Jo Laubner wurde 1952 in Stuttgart geboren. 1974 begann er Produktdesign an der Hochschule für Gestaltung in Offenbach zu studieren, wo er auch 1979 sein Diplom erwarb. Auf seinem Spezialgebiet, dem "gedeckten Tisch", arbeitete er mit vielen bekannten deutschen Firmen zusammen. Für die Firma WMF entwarf er diverse Produkte aus Edelstahl. 1989 kam die Firma Hutschenreuther hinzu.

Schon seit 1979 erarbeitet er Ausstellungs- und Interieurkonzepte für den Bundesverband Kunsthandwerk, Messe Service Gesellschaft, Frankfurt und das Bundesministerium für Wirtschaft in Bonn. Weitere Konzeptideen verwirklichte er 1989 für George Little Management, New York, Kadoke Display, Ontario und PAAS, Paris Ateliers D`Art Show. Im Frühjahr 1992 nahm er zum ersten Mal an der Triennale in Mailand teil.

Die Arbeit von Jo Laubner wurde 1983 und 1985 vom Design Center Stuttgart und 1984 auf der "10. Biennal of Industrial Design" ausgezeichnet.

Jo Laubner was born in Stuttgart in 1952. In 1974 he started studying product design at the Offenbach College of Design, graduating in 1979. He collaborates with numerous renowned German companies in his specialist area, namely the "laid table". He designed various high-grade steel products for WMF.
In 1989 he also started working for Hutschenreuther.

As early as 1979 he began developing exhibition and interior designs for the German association of Decorativ Art, trade fair operators Messe Service Gesellschaft, Frankfurt, and the Federal Ministry of Economics in Bonn. He also developed concepts in 1989 for George Little Management, New York, Kadoke Display, Ontario and PAAS, Paris Ateliers D'Art Show. In early 1992 he took part for the first time in the Triennale di Milano.

Jo Laubner's work has received awards from the Design Center Stuttgart (in 1983 and 1985) from the 10th Biennial of Industrial Design, 1984.

Der deutsche Designer Jo Laubner liebt die Ironie, das Augenzwinkern. Ihm muß Design Spaß machen. Für seinen Kunden WMF entwarf er eine Espressomaschine, die dem türkischen Mokka näher zu stehen scheint, als dem italienischen Espresso. Ein türkischer Halbmond dient als Griff für die Kanne und wieder ein kleiner, goldener Halbmond krönt den Deckel.

Trotz seiner kurzfristigen Absage an den italienischen Espresso hat Jo Laubner große Sympathien für Italien. Er schätzt die Leichtigkeit des italienischen Designs und den Mut, mit dem italienische Fabrikanten auch gewagte Entwürfe umsetzen. Dieses Interesse hat sich in seiner italophilen Formsprache niedergeschlagen.

Die additive Gestaltungstechnik von Alchimia und Memphis und natürlich der Postmoderne wendet er in seinen Entwürfen für Sektkühler und andere Edelstahlprodukte an. Darüber hinaus sucht er die Nähe zu Formen des Art-Decos und der amerikanischen Hochhausarchitektur der 30er Jahre.

Seine Entwürfe sollen sich nicht unsichtbar machen, sich nicht einer Funktion unterordnen. Vielmehr wünscht Jo Laubner, daß man eine persönliche Beziehung zu seinen Produkten entwickelt, sie ganz einfach gerne hat.

Champagnerkühler in Kegelform.
Conical champagne-cooler.

Jo Laubner loves irony, loves designing with his tongue in cheek, loves designing as long as it is fun. On behalf of WMF he designed an expresso machine which seems to be more indebted to Turkish coffee than to Italian espresso. The pot has a Turkish crescent moon as its handle, and a small golden crescent moon crowns the lid.

Despite this temporary renunciation of Italian espresso, Jo Laubner greatly appreciates Italy. He values the airy ease of Italian design highly, not to mention the courage with which Italian manufacturers are prepared to put daring projects into practice. And this interest is strongly reflected in the italophile forms he devises.

He exploits the additive approach to design so typical of Alchimia, Memphis and, of course, post-modernism as a whole in his drafts for champagne-coolers and other high-grade steel products. Moreover, he tries to find shapes that resemble both art deco forms as well as those developed as part of U.S. sky-rise architecture in the 1930s.

Laubner does not intend his designs to vanish behind or subordinate themselves to the function to which they are to be put. Rather, what he wants is for the user to develop a quite personal relationship to his products, simply to enjoy them.

Rechts: Wasserkessel, 1989.
Unten rechts: Espressokanne "Luna".
Unten links: Champagnerkühler "Frankfurter Freiheit", 1988.
Alle Produkte wurden für die Firma WMF entworfen.
Right: Kettle, 1989.
Below right: "Luna" espresso coffee pot.
Below left: "Frankfurt Freedom", champagne-cooler, 1988.
All products designed for WMF.

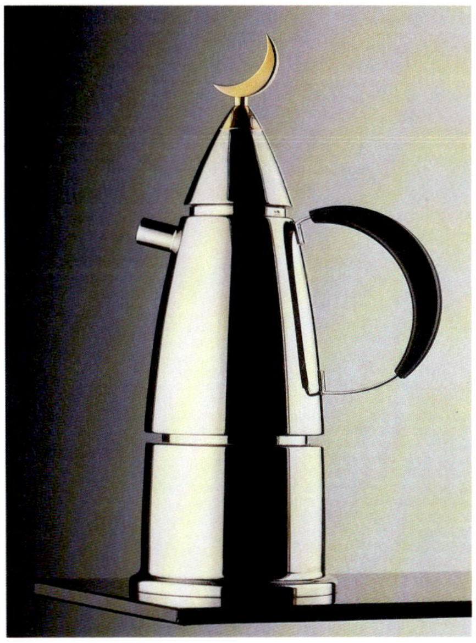

1. 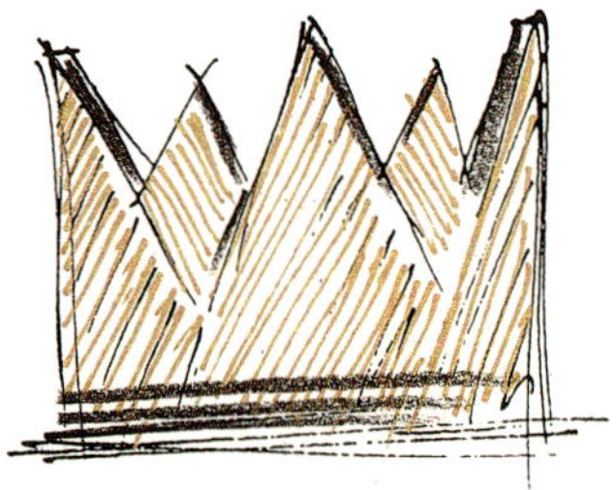

MASTER CROWN

2. 

FREEDOM

3. 

PRINCESS CROWN

4. 

CHILDREN'S CROWN

5. 

DARLING

6. 

SOTTSASS CROWN

7. 

CROWN OF LATE KING

8. 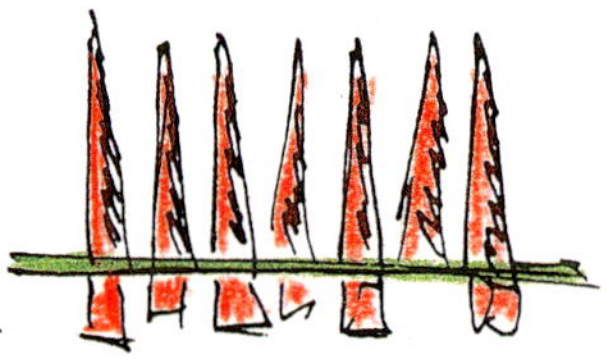

CROWN OF INDIA

9. 

ALPIN CROWN

10. 

CROWN OF LUMUMBA

11. 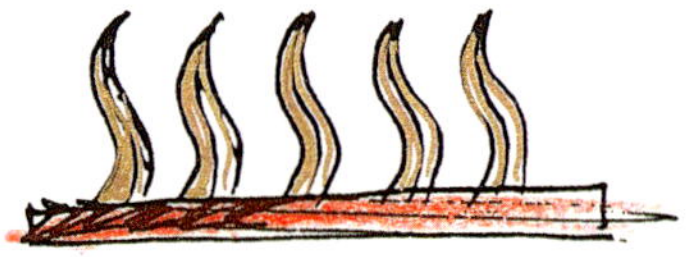

ISLAMIC CROWN

12. 

MEDUSA CROWN
WOTAN'S CROWN
CATCH THE CROWN OF BULL....
BIG BULL OF MINOS

Er ist überzeugt, daß "die Sehnsucht nach Romantik in einer hochtechnifizierten Welt zur Notwendigkeit geworden ist".

In diesem Zusammenhang sind auch seine Skizzen, Variationen und Reflektionen über den Mythos der Krone zu sehen, die für den Workshop "Colour Comedies" entstanden. Die Idee zur Krone entstand auch im Hinblick auf die Historie der Fürstenfamilie zu Ysenburg und Büdingen, den Besitzern der Waechtersbacher Keramik seit deren Gründung vor 160 Jahren.

"In fast theatralischer Art und Weise präsentiert sich das Objekt als Schale", erklärt Jo Laubner zu den beiden realisierten Entwürfen namens "Big Bull of Minos". "Reich verzierte Kronendetails werden zur machtvollen Bullenzacke."

He is convinced that "the yearning for Romanticism has become a necessity in a highly technological world."

The sketches, variations and reflections on the myth of the crown that he dreamed up for the "Colour Comedies" Workshop are to be seen in this context. The idea of the crown occured to him in connection with the long family history of the Princey of Ysenburg und Büdingen, who have owned Waechtersbacher Keramik since the company was founded 160 years ago.

"The object shows itself to be a bowl in an almost theatrical manner," explains Jo Laubner when discussing the two designs implemented under the title of "Big Bull of Minos". "Highly ornate details of the crown become powerful bull's horns."

"Big Bull of Minos, von königlicher Pracht zu archaischer Macht..."

"Big Bull of Minos, from royal glory to archaic power..."

"Reich verzierte Kronendetails werden zur machtvollen Bullenzacke."

"Highly ornate details of the crown become powerful bull horns."

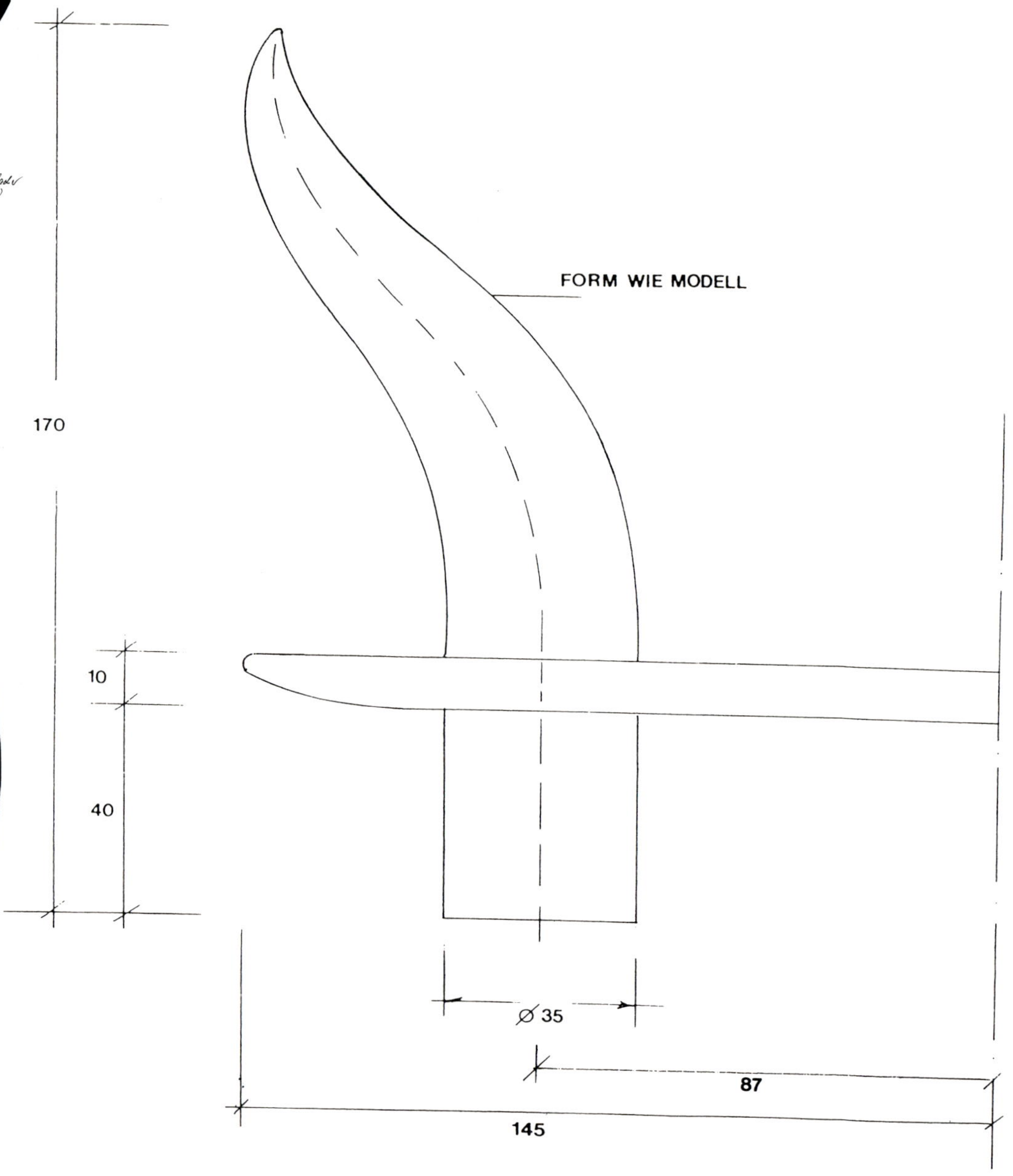

"Big Bull of Minos, der tischkrönende Akt vollzieht sich im Bewußtsein mythologischer Kraft."
"Big Bull of Minos, the crowning table act occurs with an awareness of mythological power."

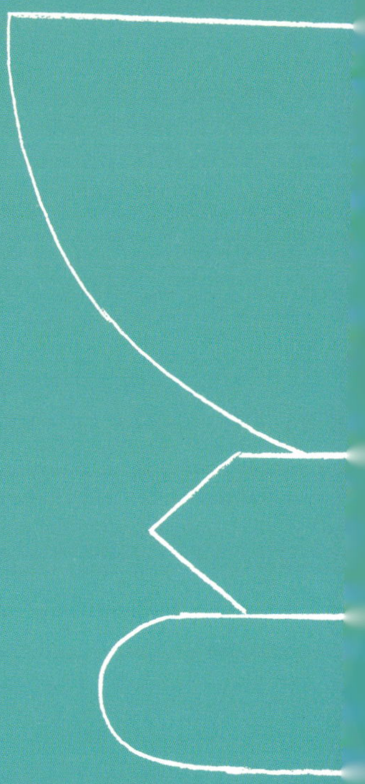

SOTTSASS
91

ETTORE SOTTSASS

Ettore Sottsass wurde 1917 in Innsbruck geboren. 1934 begann er am Turiner Polytechnikum mit dem Architekturstudium, das er 1939 abschloß.

Schon in seinen ersten Publikationen aus dem Jahre 1939 wurde deutlich, daß seine Architekturauffassung nicht mit den Ideen der funktionalistischen, modernen Architektur korrespondierte. Vielmehr wurde es zum Anspruch von Ettore Sottsass, mit Farbe, Spaß und Symbolismus die gestalterischen Problematiken zu lösen.

Auf der Triennale in Mailand war Ettore Sottsass zum ersten Mal 1947 vertreten. Er nahm 1972 an der großen Ausstellung zum italienischen Design "Italy – The new domestic landscape" im Museum of Modern Art in New York teil.

Die äußerst fruchtbare Zusammenarbeit mit der Olivetti S.p.A. begann 1958. Sottsass, der zu diesem Zeitpunkt zum ersten Mal als Industriedesigner arbeitete, erhielt den Status eines Designberaters. Die rote Schreibmaschine "Valentine", die er 1969 für Olivetti entwickelte, ist noch immer sein bekanntester Produktentwurf. Gemeinsam mit den jungen Architekten Aldo Cibic, Matteo Thun und Marco Zanini eröffnete er1980 das Designstudio "Sottsass Associati". 1981 gründete sich die Gruppe "Memphis", deren unbestrittener Kopf er bis zu seinem Austritt 1985 blieb.1986 wandte sich Sottsass Architekturprojekten zu. Es entstanden verschiedene Gebäude in Colorado, USA.

Ettore Sottsass was born in Innsbruck in 1917. In 1934 he started studying architecture at the Turin Polytechnic, graduating five years later.

The very first articles he published in 1939 already evince a conception of architecture that by no means matches the ideas of functionalist or modernist architecture. Rather, Ettore Sottsass has endeavoured ever since to solve design questions by the use of colour, symbols, and playfulness.

Ettore Sottsass first participated in the Milan Triennial in 1947, and 1972 saw his work on display at the major exhibition of Italian design at the Museum of Modern Art in New York.

Sottsass' exceptionally fruitful collaboration with Olivetti S.p.A commenced in 1958 when he was taken on as a design consultant – at a point in his career when he was working for the first time as an industrial designer. Today, "Valentine", a red typewriter which he developed for Olivetti in 1969, is still one of the most famous products he has designed. In 1981, together with the young architects Aldo Cibi, Matteo Thun and Marco Zanini he founded the "Memphis" group, of which he was the undisputed mastermind until quitting in 1985. Since 1986 Sottsass has been focusing on architectural projects and several buildings have already been constructed in Colorado, USA.

In den Mittelpunkt der praktischen und theoretischen Arbeit stellt der italienische Architekt und Designer Ettore Sottsass den Menschen. Das ist nicht neu, aber seine Forderung ist radikal: "Es sollte keine Häuser geben, sondern nur noch Menschen". Der Designer, der sich auch als Theoretiker einen Namen gemacht hat, ist heute über 70 Jahre alt und eine lebende Legende des Design.

Der gesamte Werdegang von Sottsass wurde durch seine heftige Ablehnung des Funktionalismus geprägt. Er möchte nicht Produkte gestalten, die sich unterordnen, sich an ihre Funktion unauffällig anpassen, sondern er möchte Gegenstände schaffen, die Raum und Anstoß zu einer Auseinandersetzung bieten.

Bei der Entwicklung seiner Ideen nimmt er nichts als gegeben an. Regeln und Gewohnheiten bestehen für ihn lediglich, um ihnen Alternativen gegenüberstellen zu können.
Mit Ettore Sottsass begann die Auflösung der Grenze zwischen Kunst und Design. Er versteht Gestaltung nicht als bloße stilistische Geste, sondern als konzeptionelle Arbeit. Die Formgebung hat für ihn die Funktion eines Kommunikationsmittlers zwischen Mensch und gegenständlicher Welt.

Inspirationen für seinen Gestaltungsstil fand er auf ausgedehnten Reisen durch die USA, 1956 und Indien, 1961.

Schreibmaschine "Valentine", entworfen 1969 für die Olivetti S.p.A.
"Valentine" typewriter, designed for Olivetti S.p.A. in 1969.

Besteck aus Silber, "Nuova Milano", 1990, hergestellt von Alessi.
"Nuova Milano" cutlery in silver, 1990, manufactured by Alessi.

Ettore Sottsass, Italian architect and designer, takes the human being as the central pivot of all his practical and theoretical work. That may in itself be nothing new, yet the demand he raises is a radical one: "There shouldn't really be any houses. There should only be people." Today Sottsass, who also made his name as a theoretician, is over 70 years old, a living legend of design.

Sottsass' entire development has been shaped by his vehement rejection of functionalism. He is not interested in designing subservient products which inconspicuously subordinate themselves to their function. What he wants is to create objects which provide the space and the stimulus for intellectual confrontation.

When developing his ideas he takes nothing for granted. For him, rules and conventions exist solely in order that he might pose alternatives to them.

The name Ettore Sottsass stands at the beginning of the tendency to erase the dividing line between art and design. He regards design not as a mere stylistic gesture but rather as work in the domain of concepts. The function of design as he sees it is to act as a vehicle of communication between human beings and the world of objects.

Extensive travels across the United States (in 1956) and India (in 1961) provided the sources of inspiration for his particular style.

Die Vasen "Cinira", "Eloride", "Atamante" und "Iasa" entwarf Sottsass 1986 für die "Memphis"-Kollektion.
Auch die beiden Vasen "Clesitera" und "Maia" wurden 1986 für "Memphis" entworfen.

Sottsass designed the vases "Cinira", "Eloride", "Atamante" and "Iasa" in 1986 for the Memphis collection.
The vases "Clesitera" and "Maia" were also designed for "Memphis" in 1986.

"Wolf-House", 1986, Colorado.
"Wolf House", 1986, Colorado.

Bar "Zibibbo", 1989, Fukuoka,Japan.
"Zibibbo" bar, 1989, Fukuoka, Japan.

In den Vereinigten Staaten faszinierte ihn die "American Culture", die Massenmedien und die Gegenwart lauter und schriller Farben. Während seines Aufenthaltes lernte er den Abstrakten Expressionismus und die Pop Art kennen. Beide Kunstrichtungen hatten Einfluß auf seinen Gestaltungsstil. Gerade die Inspiration durch die Pop Art ist den Arbeiten von Ettore Sottsass noch bis zum heutigen Tage anzumerken.

Während seiner langen Reise durch Indien fand Sottsass wieder andere Anstöße, die er bereit war, aufzunehmen. Von großem Interesse war für ihn der bewußte Umgang der Inder mit ihren Alltags-Gegenständen. Die Inder meinen, so erkärt Sottsass, "daß der Gegenstand immer ein Platz mit einer rituellen Eigenschaft ist: Erst einmal im Raum aufgestellt, wird der Gegenstand direkt ein Werkzeug für den rituellen Gebrauch. Die Art, wie die Inder den Gegenstand betrachten, unterscheidet sich gänzlich von der Betrachtungsweise, wie wir sie gewöhnt sind."

Stehlampe "Callimaco", Artemide.
"Callimaco" standard lamp, Artemide.

"Carlton" Raumteiler, 1981, Memphis.
"Carlton" room divider, 1981, Memphis.

In the United States, what fascinated him was "American Culture", the mass media and the presence of loud, garish colours. During his stay there, he became acquainted with the work of abstract expressionism and Pop Art. Both art currents were to influence his style of design. Echoes of Pop Art in particular can be detected in the works of Ettore Sottsass right through to the present day.

On his long journey through India, Sottsass encountered, and was willing to embrace, a different set of stimuli. He was greatly impressed by the awareness which characterizes the Indians' relationship to their everyday objects. The Indians, Sottsass explains, have a habit "of thinking that the object is always a location with a ritual quality: once it has been placed in space, the object immediately becomes an instrument for ritual use. The approach taken by these Indians vis-à-vis the object is entirely different from the one we are used to."

"Manchmal kann eine Linie schief sein. Das macht aber nichts: die durch sie verwirklichten Gegenstände bekommen Leben, weil sie wirklich verstanden, erlebt werden."[8] Es sind die Geheimnisse dieser Kultur, die er entdecken und vermitteln möchte.
Auch in der späten Phase seiner Karriere sucht Sottsass immer wieder die Auseinandersetzung mit aktuellen Design-Tendenzen und arbeitet dabei mit Designern zusammen, die zum Teil beträchtlich jünger sind als er selbst.

Aus diesem Interesse für junge Designtendenzen heraus, begann er 1979 bei der Designergruppe "Alchimia" mitzuarbeiten, die er bald wieder verließ. Mit drei sehr jungen Designern als Partnern gründete er 1980 das Büro "Sottsass Associati". In diesem Zusammenhang muß unbedingt die Designer-Gruppe "Memphis" erwähnt werden, deren Gründungsmitglied er war. Ettore Sottsass galt als unermüdlicher Motor und als alles verbindende Kraft innerhalb dieser Bewegung. "Memphis" gab neben der Postmoderne die wichtigsten Impulse für das Design der 80er Jahre.

Die Espressotasse wird zur Skulptur...
The espresso cup becomes sculpture...

"Sometimes a line may be crooked, but that doesn't matter: the things they have created come to life, because they are really understood, really experienced." It is this culture's secrets which he sets out to discover and convey.

Even in the latter phase of his career, Sottsass is continually seeking to come to terms with current design trends, choosing to work with designers considerably younger than himself.

This interest in young design trends led him to join the "Alchimia" designers in 1979, only to leave the group soon afterwards in order to found "Sottsass Associati" in 1980 in partnership with three very young designers. No account of Sottsass' career would be complete without mention here of the "Memphis" group of designers, of which he was a founder member. Ettore Sottsass was regarded as the movement's indefatigable driving force and provider of the cohesive energy drawing together all its various currents. It was "Memphis", alongside Post-Modernism, that gave 1980s design its most important impetus.

...das Espressotrinken wird zum Ritus.

...drinking espresso becomes a rite.

Milchkaffee- und Teetasse. Alltägliche Gefäße werden zu Kultgegenständen stilisiert.
The tea bowl rests on a pedestal. The influence of White coffee cup and teacup. Everyday receptacles are stylized into cultic objects.

Das Ziel der "Memphis" Bewegung war es, die Person des Designers aus dem industriellen Kontext zu lösen. Der so von externen Maßgaben befreite Designer gestaltet Produkte, die er selbst gerne besitzen würde. Er spielt mit Dekoren, Farben und Formen.

Innerhalb dieser Gruppe konnte Ettore Sottsass seinen Gestaltungsanspruch voll verwirklichen. Er entwarf Produkte, wie beispielsweise den Raumteiler "Carlton" (s. Abb. S.53), die durch ihren Reichtum an Dekoren und Farben ein Eigenleben entwickelten und so zu einer Skulptur im Hause ihres Besitzers wurden.

Für den Workshop "Colour Comedies" hat sich Ettore Sottsass nicht zum ersten Mal mit der farbigen Keramik auseinandergesetzt, schon seit Beginn seiner Karriere hat er sich immer wieder diesem Material zugewandt. Denn gerade im Umgang mit diesem alten und traditionsreichen Material gelingt es Sottsass, den Objekten eine symbolische Kraft mit auf den Weg zu geben, die für seine Arbeit so wichtig und bezeichnend ist. Auf seine Keramiken und Möbel angesprochen, erklärte Ettore Sottsass einmal: "ich hoffe z.B., daß, wenn jemand ein Zimmer betritt, in welchem eines meiner Gläser steht, der Betreffende fühlt, in diesem Raum befindet sich ein sonderbares Objekt, falls diese Reaktion eintreten sollte, wäre das schon ein wunderbares Ergebnis."[9]

The aim of the "Memphis" movement was to detach the designer from the industrial context. Thus freed from external constraints, the designer is able to create products that he would like to own himself. He is at liberty to play with decor, with colours and forms.

Within this group, Ettore Sottsass was able to realize his designing ideal to the full. He designed products, like the "Carlton" room divider (see ill. p 53), whose richness of decor and colour gave them a life of their own, becoming sculptures in the houses of their owners.

Ettore Sottsass' contributions to the "Colour Comedies" Workshop are by no means his first encounter with coloured ceramics. It is a medium to which Sottsass has returned again and again since the earliest day of his career. For it is using precisely this ancient and highly traditional material that Sottsass is best able to instill in his objects that symbolic force which is such an important, such a characteristic feature of his work. He has designed a number of earthenware receptacles. Questioned about his ceramics and furniture, Sottsass once explained: "I hope, for example, that, when someone enters a room in which one of my glasses stands, that the person in question feels 'there is a uniquely strange object in this room'. It would be marvellous if this were to be the reaction."[9]

Die einfache Trinkschale ruht auf einem Sockel. Der Akt des Trinkens wird erhöht und zelebriert.
The simple drinking bowl rests on a pedestal. The act of drinking is exalted and celebrated.

Um die verschiedenen Objekte zu erhalten, mußten unzählige Formen erstellt und wochenlange Versuche in der Glasurenentwicklung durchgeführt werden.

Manufacturing the various objects required the construction of countless moulds and weeks of experimentation with different glazes.

Die Obstschale wird zur Säule, die sich dem Betrachter entgegenreckt und ihre Früchte feilbietet. Ein Objekt, das in einer schönen Form vom Präsentieren und Darbieten erzählt.

The fruit bowl becomes a column, reaching up towards the beholder and offering its fruit. The aesthetic form of this object becomes an eloquent image of presentation as such.

"...in diesem Raum befindet sich ein sonderbares Objekt."

"...there is a uniquely strange object in this room."

WAECHTERSBACHER KERAMIK

Wächtersbach

WAECHTERSBACH

WBACH

Wächtersbach

Ansicht der Fabrik vor 1870, nach einer zeitgenössischen Lithographie.
View of the factory prior to 1870, from a contemporary lithograph.

Die Waechtersbacher Keramik wurde am 08. Juni 1932 im "Schlierbacher Grund" nahe dem Ort Wächtersbach von Graf Adolf zu Ysenburg und Büdingen und sechs Teilhabern gegründet. Noch in demselben Jahr konnte man erfolgreich mit der Herstellung keramischer Gebrauchsgegenstände beginnen, die von Anfang an durch eine allgemein beliebte Formgebung und durch eine besonders sorgfältige Verarbeitung eine von der üblichen Fertigung abweichende Note erzielten.

Bald nach der Gründung übernahm Graf zu Ysenburg durch Investitionen in den Ausbau der Fabrik alle Anteile. Der Bau der Eisenbahnlinie Hanau-Wächtersbach bereits 1864 öffnete neue Märkte und verhalf dem Unternehmen schnell zu Wachstum und Bekanntheit über die Landesgrenzen hinaus. Eine besondere Hochblüte erlebte die Waechtersbacher Keramik schon zur Jahrhundertwende. 1903 wurde ein "Kunstatelier" eingerichtet, in welchem so namhafte Gestalter wie Neureuther, Behrens, Christiansen und Olbrich eine Vielzahl von Meisterwerken schufen.

Heute werden diese Gestalter zu den renommiertesten Künstlern des Jugendstils gezählt. Ihre Arbeiten bestachen durch einen unnachahmlichen Farben- und Dekorcharakter und gaben der farbigen Keramik von Waechtersbach neue individuelle Impulse. Viele Arbeiten aus dieser Zeit sind heute im Museum der Fabrik und in den Museen in aller Welt zu besichtigen.

Heute gehört die Waechtersbacher Keramik zu den bedeutendsten Keramik-Produzenten in Europa und genießt weltweit einen ausgezeichneten Ruf als Hersteller von Geschirr und Geschenkartikeln aus hochwertigem Hartsteingut, insbesondere als Trendsetter für farbige, junge und modische Dekore.

Charakter und Vielfalt des Sortiments werden bestimmt von der Anwendung verschiedener Dekor-Techniken. Die Waechtersbacher Keramik, das sind vor allem 480 Menschen. Auch heute noch werden viele wesentliche Arbeiten in der Produktion von Hand ausgeführt. Nur auf diese Weise erhalten wir ein überzeugendes Produkt, das höchsten Ansprüchen an die Qualität, an die Verarbeitung und an die Brillanz der Glasuren und Farben gerecht wird.

Zu der Fabrik bei Waechtersbach gehören ein vor 16 Jahren errichtetes modernes Werk in Spanien, sowie eigene Vertriebsgesellschaften in Großbritannien und den USA.
Das Unternehmen befindet sich nun in der 6. Generation der Familie des Fürsten zu Ysenburg und Büdingen.

Teeservice "Dresden", Entwurf: Schweitzer um 1912.
"Dresden" tea service, designed by Schweitzer ca.1912.

Vase für langstielige Blumen, Modell: Olbrich 1901, Dekor Neureuther 1902.
Vase for long-stemmed flowers, model: olbrich, 1901, decor: Neureuther, 1902.

Deckeldose, Entwurf Albin Müller. Marke: Kunstabteilung Neureuther, um 1915.
Bowl with lid, designed by Albin Müller. Mark: Neureuther Art Department, ca. 1915.

On 8th June, 1832, at a place called "Schlierbacher Grund" near Waechtersbach, Count Adolf of Ysenburg und Büdingen, together with six partners, founded Waechtersbacher Keramik. That same year, the firm successfully began producing ceramic objects of everyday use. Right from the earliest days, their generally popular design and the quality of the workmanship placed them in a category of their own.

It was not long before all shares passed into the hands of Count Ysenburg, who invested in extensions to the factory. The completion of the Hanau-Wächtersbach railway line as early as 1864 opened up new markets, bringing rapid prosperity to the company and extending its reputation beyond the state borders of Hessen. The turn of the century was a heyday of Waechtersbacher Keramik. In 1903 an "art studio" was inaugurated, and it was here that such distinguished designers as Neureuther, Behrens, Christiansen and Olbrich created numerous masterpieces.

Today these artists are remembered as leading figures of the Art Nouveau movement. What made their pieces stand out was their inimitable use of colour and decoration, and each left an individual mark on Waechterbacher's colourful ceramics. Many objects dating from this period are on view today in the factory museum and in museums around the world.

Waechtersbacher Keramik is today one of Europe's leading ceramics producers. Throughout the world Waechtersbacher is renowned as a producer of high quality porcelain tableware and household articles, and is particularly associated with trendsetting designs, with youthfulness and colour.

What makes the Waechtersbacher range so rich in character and variety is the number of different decorative techniques employed. Above all, Waechtersbacher Keramik means 480 people. Even today, many of the crucial stages of the production process are still carried out by hand. This is the only way of ensuring that the quality, the workmanship, and the brilliance of the glazes and colours live up to the high standards that can be expected of a superior product.

In addition to the factory near Wächtersbach, the company operates a modern plant in Spain, built 16 years ago, and runs its own marketing subsidiaries in Britain and the United States. Ownership of the firm has now been in the family of Prince Ysenburg und Büdingen for six generations.

Farbenprächtiges handgestempeltes Geschirr-Service "Valencia" aus dem aktuellen Programm, 1992.
"Valencia", a richly coloured, hand-stamped tableware service, belonging to the currently available range, 1992.

BIBLIOGRAFIE / *BIBLIOGRAPHY*

Bellaty, Nally: Neues Italienisches Design, Piere Terrail 1992. Originalausgabe: New Italian Design, Rizzoli International Publications, New York, 1990.

Botand, Bogmar:The Japanese Architecture, Rizzoli International Publications Inc., New York. p. 204 ff.

Calloway, Stephen; Baudot, Francois; Lemaire, Gerard-Georges; Elizabeth Garouste et Mattia Bonetti, Michel Aveline Editeur 1990.

Collins, Michael: Design und Postmoderne. Droemersche Verlagsanstalt Th. Knaur Nachf., München 1990. Originalausgabe: Academy Editions 1989.

De Bure, Gilles: Ettore Sottsass Jnr.; Rivage, Marseille, 1987.

Hofstede ter Poul: Memphis 1981 - 1988. Groninger Museum, 1989.

Horn, Richard: Memphis - Objects, Furniture and Patterns, Fire Side Book, Simon & Schuster Inc., New York 1986.

G.A. Architect, 5: Zaha Hadid. A.D.A. Edita, Tokyo, 1986. Reprint 1990.

Ikon-Gallerie:" Ettore Sottsass-Zeichnungen aus 4 Jahrzehnten", 1990.

Kerstenbaum, Jackie: Emerging Japanese Architects of the 1990s. Columbia University Press, New York, 1991.

Lisitzky-Küppers, Sophie: El Lisitzky. VEB Verlag der Kunst Dresden 1967 in einer Neuauflage der Büchergilde Gutenberg, 1980.

Sottsass Associati, Rizzoli International Publications Inc., New York, 1988.

Sparke, Penny: Ettore Sottsass Jnr.; The Design Council 1982.

Architecture Cree: Minato Ward. October/November 1987, pp. 142 - 145.

Architektur und Wohnen: Atsushi Kitagawara; gebäude die keine Antwort geben. Februar 1989.

Art: Ein Schuß Poesie gehört zum Design. Februar 1992.

Brown, Leigh: Disney Deco. The New York Times, April 8, 1990.

Filer, Martin: A Shrine to Wine. House and Garden, September 1987.

Goldberger, Paul: Architecture of a Different Color. New York Times Magazine, October 10, 1982.

Goldberger, Paul: Rising the Architectural Ante In California. The New York Times, Sunday, October 14, 1990.

Levene, Richard C; Márquez Cecilia, Fernando: Zaha Hadid 1983/1991. El Croquis, 52, Diciembre Enero.

Sottsass, Ettore: Experience with Ceramics. Domus 489, August 1970.

The Japanese Architect No. 339. Miaon-kaku. July 1985, pp. 25 - 31.

Viladas, Pillar: The Taste of a Tastemaker, Progressive Architecture, September, 1988.

Quellennachweis *Sources*

1 Stephen Calloway, Francois Baudot, Gerard-Georges Lemaire: "Elizabeth Garouste et Mattia Bonetti". Michael Aveline Editeur, 1990. Christian Lacroix pp./s. 188/189.

2 Paul Goldberger: "Architecture of a Different Color". New York Times Magazine, October 10, 1982.

3 Paul Goldberger: "Architecture of a Different Color". New York Times Magazine, October 10, 1982.

4 Richard Levene, Fernando Márquez: Zaha Hadid 1983/1991. El Croquis, 52 "Entrevista con Zaha Hadid"/"Interview with Zaha Hadid" p./s. 13.

5 Richard Levene, Fernando Márquez: Zaha Hadid 1993/1991. El Croquis, 52 "Entrevista con Zaha Hadid"/"Interview with Zaha Hadid" p./s. 13.

6 Architektur und Wohnen: "Atsushi Kitagawara: Der Surrealist". 02/89.

7 Jacky Kerstenbaum: "Emerging Japanese Architects of the 1990s". Columbia University Press, New York 1991.

8 Poul ter Hofstede (Editor/Redaktion) "Memphis 1981-1988". Gian Piero Vincenzo: "Interview Ettore Sottsass". Groninger Museum 1989, pp. 8/9, pp./s. 22/23.

9 Ikon-Gallerie: "Ettore Sottsass-Zeichnungen aus 4 Jahrzehnten", Rainer Krause/Ettore Sottsass "10 Fragen und 10 Antworten" "10 Questions and 10 Answers", 1990, p./s. 39.

Fotonachweis *Photo Credits*

Seite/Page 7: Dirk Bleicker

Seite/Page 9: Simon Kentish

Seite/Page 10: Karin Knoblich,
Links unten, *lower left*: Volker Albus

Seite/Page 11: Karin Knoblich

Seite/Page 19: Stephen Barker

Seite/Page 20 Oben, *top*: Steven Brooke,
unten, *bottom:* William Taylor,
Tishman Reality & Construction Company

Seite/Page 21 Oben,*top*: Steuben,
Mitte, *centre*: William Taylor,
Unten, *bottom*: Markuse Corporation.

Seite/Page 25: James Horner

Seite/Page 26: Edra

Seite/Page 27: Paul Warchol

Seite/Page 36 Oben,*top*: Shinkenchiku, Mitsuo Matsuoka,
Unten, *bottom:* Shinkenchiku, Shigeo Ogawa.

Seite/Page 37: Shigeru Ohno

Seite/Page 42/43: WMF

Seite/Page 49: Gitty Darugar

Seite/Page 50 Oben, *top*: Sottsass Associati,
Unten, bottom: Alessi

Seite/Page 51: Santi Caleca

Seite/Page 52: Oben, *top*: Santi Caleca,
Unten,bottom: Nacasa & Partners

Seite/Page 53: Aldo Ballo

Seite/Page 60 Unten, *bottom*: Heinz und *and* Lilo Frensch

Seite/Page 61 Links oben, *upper left*: Heinz und *and* Lilo Frensch,
Rechts unten, *lower right*: Wolfgang Schmidt, Jens Grundmann

DANK / *THANKS*

Vielen Dank den Mitarbeitern der Waechtersbacher Keramik, die dieses Projekt mit Ihrem Sachverständnis und ihrem großen, persönlichen Einsatz erst ermöglicht haben.

We would like to express our gratitude of the employees of Waechtersbacher Keramik, without whose expertise and outstandig personal commitment this project would not have been possible.

Karin Gold	Sekretärin	*Karin Gold*	*secretary*
Gerd Hausen	Kerammodelleur	*Gerd Hausen*	*ceramics modeller*
Hans Horstmann	Kerammaler	*Hans Horstmann*	*ceramics painter*
Walter Koziolek	Dekorationsleiter	*Walter Koziolek*	*decoration supervisor*
Katrin Nawothnig	Dip. Ing. Keramik	*Katrin Nawothnig*	*chatered ceramics engineer*
Klaus Nawothnig	Geschäftsführer Technik	*Klaus Nawothnig*	*technical director*
Burkhardt Paus	Betriebsassistent	*Burkhardt Paus*	*junior works manager*
Willi Schuch	Kerammaler	*Willi Schuch*	*ceramics painter*
Herbert Seibel	Kerammaler	*Herbert Seibel*	*ceramics painter*
Peter Seifert	Kerammodelleur	*Peter Seifert*	*ceramics modeller*
Claudia Trampen	Produktmanagerin	*Claudia Trampen*	*product manager*
Angelika Trupp	Kerammalerin	*Angelika Trupp*	*ceramics painter*
Gabi Trupp	Kerammalerin	*Gabi Trupp*	*ceramics painter*
Monika Wittmann	Kerammalerin	*Monika Wittmann*	*ceramics painter*